Great Creatures of the World

DOLPHINS
AND PORPOISES

Ian Beames/Ardea London

Dean Lee

David Gaskin

Pat Morris/Ardea London Ltd

R.S. Wells

Graeme Ellis

Great Creatures of the World

DOLPHINS
AND PORPOISES

Facts On File

New York • Oxford • Sydney

Dolphins and Porpoises
A Great Creatures of the World book

Facts On File, Inc.   Facts On File Limited
460 Park Avenue South   or   Collins Street
New York NY 10016   Oxford OX4 1XJ
USA   United Kingdom

Ben Cropp

Written by Janelle Hatherly and Delia Nicholls

Consulting Editor: Professor M.M. Bryden
DSc FAIBiol
Professor of Veterinary
Anatomy, University of Sydney,
Australia

Adapted from material supplied by:

Dr Lawrence G. Barnes, curator and head,
Vertebrate Paleontology Section, Natural History
Museum of Los Angeles County, Los Angeles,
California, USA

Professor M.M. Bryden, professor of veterinary anatomy, University of Sydney, Australia

Peter Corkeron, research assistant, Department of
Veterinary Anatomy, University of Sydney, Australia

Carson Creagh, editor and natural history writer,
Sydney, Australia

Dr W.H. Dawbin, honorary research associate, Australian Museum, Sydney

Hugh Edwards, marine photographer and author,
Perth, Western Australia

Dr R. Ewan Fordyce, senior lecturer, Department of
Geology, University of Otago, New Zealand

Sir Richard Harrison, Emeritus professor of
anatomy, University of Cambridge, UK, Honorary
Fellow, Downing College, Cambridge, United
Kingdom

Kaiya Zhou, professor and dean, Department of
Biology, Nanjing Normal University, Nanjing,
People's Republic of China

Dr Victor Manton, curator, Whipsnade Park,
Dunstable, Bedfordshire, United Kingdom

Dr Robert J. Morris, principal scientific officer,
Institute of Oceanographic Sciences, United Kingdom

Marty Snyderman, marine photographer, cinema-
tographer and author, San Diego, California, USA

Dr Ruth Thompson, author and historian, Sydney,
Australia

Facts On File books are available at special discounts
when purchased in bulk quantities for businesses,
associations, institutions or sales promotions. Please
contact the Special Sales Department of our New York
office at 212/683-2244 (dial 800/322-8755 except in
NY, AK & HI) or in Oxford at 0865 728399.

Library of Congress Cataloguing-in-Publication Data:

Hatherly, Janelle.
Dolphins and Porpoises/Janelle Hatherly and Delia
Nicholls.
p. cm. — (A Great Creatures book)
Includes index.
Summary: Describes the physical characteristics,
habits, and natural environment of dolphins and
porpoises and discusses their evolution and
relationship to human beings.
ISBN 0-8160-2272-0
1. Dolphins — Juvenile literature. 2. Porpoises —
Juvenile literature.
1. Dolphins. 2. Porpoises.
I. Nicholls, Delia. II. Title. III. Series.
QL 737.C432 H38   1990   89-34669
599..5'3 — dc 20   CIP AC
British CIP data available on request

Produced by Weldon Owen Pty Limited
43 Victoria Street, McMahons Point, NSW 2060
Telex AA23038 Fax (02) 929 8352
A member of the Weldon International Group of
Companies
Sydney • San Francisco • Hong Kong • London • Chicago

Publisher: John Owen
Publishing Manager: Stuart Laurence
Managing Editor: Beverley Barnes
Project Coordinator: Claire Craig
Picture Editor: Kathy Gerrard
Designer: Diane Quick
Maps: Greg Campbell
Illustrations: Tony Pyrzakowski
Production Director: Mick Bagnato

Typeset by Keyset Phototype
Printed by Kyodo-Shing Loong Printing Industries
Printed in Singapore

10 9 8 7 6 5 4 3 2 1

Bernd Würsig

P. Arnantho/Earthviews

Page 1: An orca shows its trainer how to do backstroke.
Page 2: When orcas "spyhop" they rise vertically above the surface of the water and investigate their surroundings.
Opposite page: A dusky dolphin demonstrates its acrobatic skills.

Francisco Erizo/Bruce Coleman Ltd

Bernd Würsig

Contents

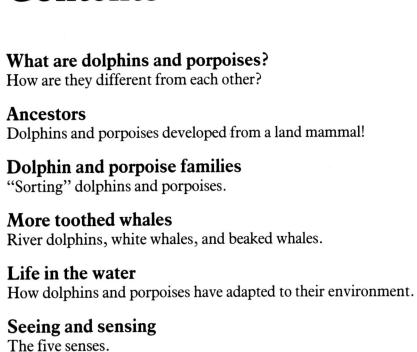

Opposite page: These bottlenose dolphins look sleek and streamlined as they move from the lighter surface waters to the darker depths of the ocean.

Rosemary Chastney/Ocean Images Inc./Planet Earth Pictures

Michael Bryden

Australian Picture Library/Volvox

Paul Ensor/Hedgehog House, New Zealand

R.J. Tomkins/Australasian Nature Transparencies

What are dolphins and porpoises?

Anyone lucky enough to watch a school of dolphins or porpoises gliding along beneath the surface of the water or leaping gracefully into the air marvels at their speed and agility. They seem to be intelligent, and they are certainly friendly. In their natural environment, or in captivity, dolphins and porpoises fascinate us.

Dolphins and porpoises are warm-blooded *mammals*. Although they live in the sea, they breathe air. They belong to a large scientific group (an *order*) called Cetacea or cetaceans. Whales also belong to this order. In fact, dolphins and porpoises are small "toothed whales." This means they are part of the same scientific group (suborder) as the whales that have teeth, for example, the sperm whale or any of the beaked whales.

The "great whales" such as the blue whale or the humpback whale do not have teeth. They have baleen (plates of horny fiber arranged on both sides of the upper jaw), which they use to filter or sieve their food. Toothed whales have one *blowhole* (a nostril or opening at the top of the head through which they breathe) while the great whales have two blowholes.

Paint a picture

When asked to describe a dolphin or a porpoise, you probably think of a gray fish-like creature with tiny eyes, a smooth, streamlined body, a flat rather large horizontal tail, and a permanent smile. It also has two side *flippers* and a fin (called a *dorsal fin*) on its back. Have you ever seen this sickle-shaped back fin cutting through the water and coming toward you at great speed? Did you think it was a shark?

Kaiya Zhou

▲ *The baiji lives in the Yangtze River in China.*

▼ *Common dolphins hunt in the open ocean and are often seen in groups of up to several hundred animals.*

Francois Gohier/Ardea London

Dolphin or porpoise?

Could you tell the difference? Unless you know a lot about dolphins and porpoises it is easy to confuse them. Usually, dolphins have beaks and more noticeable dorsal fins than porpoises. Porpoises are usually smaller than dolphins, and their teeth are spade-shaped, not pointed like dolphins' teeth.

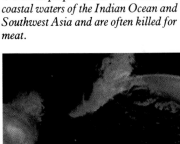

▼ *Finless porpoises live in the warm coastal waters of the Indian Ocean and Southwest Asia and are often killed for meat.*

Porpoises

Porpoises are frequently mistaken for dolphins. In the United States *all* small toothed whales are often called porpoises. But, porpoises are different from dolphins. For example, they have no distinct beak. They also have rounded heads and are usually smaller than dolphins. Porpoises have either no dorsal fin or one that is less pronounced than that of a dolphin. There are also fewer kinds of porpoises than dolphins.

One of the best-known porpoises is Dall's porpoise. It is the fastest and strongest swimmer of all toothed whales. Other kinds of porpoises are the harbor porpoise, Burmeister's porpoise, the vaquita, the spectacled porpoise, and the finless porpoise.

▼ *Dall's porpoise*

Dolphins

Dolphins have been part of our mythology and legends since about 1500 B.C. Greek and Roman artists used their images on ancient coins, mosaic floors, in paintings, and in sculpture. There are many stories of the special bond between humans and dolphins. Over the centuries some people have come to believe that dolphins are as clever as humans.

Although there are many kinds of dolphins, the best known is the common dolphin. It has been drawn by artists for many centuries.

The largest dolphin is the orca. It stands out because of its size and the bold black and white markings on its skin. It has a varied diet and likes to eat seabirds, turtles, sea lions, whales, and other dolphins and porpoises. It even eats great white sharks.

Most of the studies of dolphins have been with bottlenose dolphins because they live close to the shores of the United States, South Africa, Argentina, England, France, and Australia. They were among the first dolphins to be kept in captivity.

Most dolphins live in the sea, while some, for example, river dolphins, live only in fresh water. Others, such as the Indo-Pacific humpback dolphin, which lives in salt water, are able to move into freshwater rivers for short times only.

Ancestors

Over millions of years, dolphins and porpoises developed from land mammals. They are closely related to each other as well as being linked to those other well-known sea creatures — the great whales.

Dolphins, porpoises, and whales are mammals that live in the sea. A typical land mammal such as a dog has ears, fur, paws, and legs. It may be hard to believe, but scientists think that whales, dolphins, and porpoises *evolved* from land mammals with these features. Fossils suggest that mesonychids, hoofed, wolf-like animals about the size of a dog that lived some 50 million years ago, are their likely ancestor.

Some mesonychids, it seems, lived at the edge of the sea and fed on fish in the shallow waters. Over millions of years, their descendants spent more and more of their time in the water, and they became amphibious (able to live both in the water and on land). Eventually, they adapted totally to life in the water. Their forelimbs became short, broad paddles. Their body shapes became more streamlined as their tails flattened, and their ears, hindlimbs, and hair became less obvious. Their nostrils (or blowholes) were also located higher up the head so that they could breathe without surfacing completely. The illustrations on this page show you just how the skull of dolphins and porpoises has developed over millions of years.

About 30–40 million years ago there were many changes in the geology of the earth. New continents with new environments were formed, and two groups of cetaceans with different feeding habits evolved.

▲ *Despite their wolf-like appearance, mesonychids are believed to be the ancestors of dolphins and porpoises.*

Did you know?

About fifty million years ago, Australia and South America were joined together across Antarctica. This large land mass is called "Gondwana". When Gondwana split up, new continents and oceans were formed. The ancestors of dolphins and porpoises moved to new seas and developed new ways of feeding.

blowhole

A skull from 50 million years ago

blowhole

A skull from 45 million years ago

blowhole

A skull from 40 million years ago

blowhole

A skull from 25 million years ago

blowhole

A skull from 15 million years ago

Fossil skulls

The ancestors of dolphins and porpoises looked different, as you can see by these five skulls illustrated from fossils. Fifty million years ago mesonychids hunted land animals, and their skull and teeth were like those of other carnivorous land mammals. As they spent more time in the water, the jaw, headshape, and teeth changed to suit a diet of fish and squid. The jaw became more beaklike and the nostrils were located closer to the top of the head.

Primitive toothed whales

These are the ancestors of today's dolphins and porpoises, the sperm whales, the white whales, beaked whales, and river dolphins. Dolphins resembling the ones we know today, appeared about 15 million years ago. Porpoises separated from their dolphin-like relatives about 10 million years ago.

Primitive baleen whales

These are the ancestors of today's great whales. The first ones still had teeth, but later ones had baleen on both sides of their upper jaw. They used this baleen to sieve or filter tiny organisms from the water.

▲ *Scientists do not know for certain what the first toothed whales looked like. But they may have looked something like this.*

Shaped by the sea

The shark (a fish), the ancient ichthyosaur (a reptile) and the dolphin (a mammal) all have a similar streamlined body shape. Yet ... they all had different ancestors. Evolution is an efficient method of adapting to the environment. As the shark, ichthyosaur, and dolphin all live in the water, they have evolved a body shape that is perfectly suited to their environment.

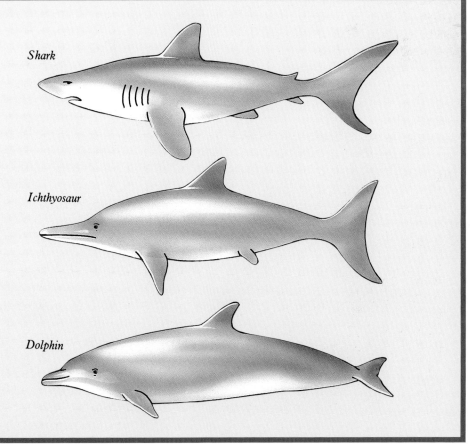

Shark

Ichthyosaur

Dolphin

Dolphin and porpoise families

Scientists have worked out classification schemes to help them sort out all the kinds of living things. In this chapter we will look at some of the different types of dolphins and porpoises.

Dolphins and porpoises belong to the class called mammals. They are related to humans, whales, dogs, and other warm-blooded animals whose young are fed with milk from special mammary glands. They have little in common with sharks and fish, which belong to different classes.

Classes are made up of orders. If you look at the table, you can see that the order Cetacea, to which whales, dolphins, and porpoises belong, is broken down into two suborders: Mysticeti (baleen whales) and Odontoceti (toothed whales). These suborders are broken down further into *families*. In this book we shall look at eight of the families in suborder Odontoceti. The sperm whale family is more "whale-like" than "dolphin-like" in size, so it has been included in *Whales*, another book in the Great Creatures series.

Each family contains one or more *genus*, which is divided into *species*, or kinds. Animals of the same species are the most closely related to each other, and only members of the same species can breed together.

ORDER	SUBORDER	FAMILY
CETACEA *Cetaceans (Whales, dolphins, and porpoises)*	***MYSTICETI*** *Baleen whales*	*Right whales*
		Pygmy right whale
		Gray whale
		Rorquals
	ODONTOCETI *Toothed whales*	*Sperm whales*
		White whales
		Beaked whales
		Dolphins and small toothed whales
		Porpoises
		River dolphins
		Amazon River dolphin
		Chinese river dolphin
		Franciscana

Hector's dolphin 5 feet (1.5 m)

Human 6 feet (2 m)

Orca 31 feet (9.5 m)

▲ *Hector's dolphin is one of the smallest dolphins. Here it is compared to a human and an orca, the largest of the dolphins.*

◀ *Spotted dolphins are about 31 inches (80 cm) when they are born, but they can grow up to 8 feet (2.5 m) long.*

Family Delphinidae

True dolphins belong to the family Delphinidae, which contains 31 species of dolphins.

Orca

This is the largest member of this family. It is often called the "killer whale." This very menacing name makes people think it is hostile and dangerous to humans. But is it? Read the last two pages of this chapter to find out.

▶ *False killer whale*

What's in a name?

Did you know that the false killer whale is actually classified as a dolphin? It is larger than most other dolphins but it is typically dolphin-like in shape. It likes to eat squid and fish, but it has been seen attacking other dolphins and sick or young humpback whales for food.

False killer whale

It sounds big and dangerous but the false killer whale is neither a whale nor a killer of humans. It is, however, one of the larger species of dolphins and males can grow up to 19.5 feet (6 m) in length. Its body is glossy black or dark gray, and unlike most members of the family Delphinidae, it has no beak. Its dorsal fin is large, and its flippers have a hump on their front edge.

False killer whales live in herds of up to several hundred animals in the open oceans of tropical and temperate regions. However, they are also well known for their mass strandings in shallow waters, when they cannot reach the safety of the open sea. They are kept successfully in captivity and can learn to do tricks if they are trained.

Common dolphin

The beautiful common dolphin is a well-known member of the family Delphinidae. It has distinctive markings, with an orange stripe on each side. A black stripe runs from the black beak to and around the eye. Its dorsal fin is sickle-shaped, and its flippers are long and slender. It can grow to about 8 feet (2.6 m) long, an average size for a dolphin.

The common dolphin is widespread in warmer temperate and tropical waters, and it lives in both shallow coastal seas and the open ocean. It feeds on anchovies, herring, sardines, and squid, and is often found accompanied by schools of tuna.

Pacific white-sided dolphin

This dolphin is closely related to the white-beaked dolphin and the Atlantic white-sided dolphin. They all belong to the genus (or group) *Lagenorhynchus*, which is the largest group in the dolphin family.

Like its close relatives, the Pacific white-sided dolphin forms very large herds. Sometimes, several thousand animals are seen traveling together. This dolphin loves to ride the waves of ships' bows. It has a stocky body, a tall sickle-shaped dorsal fin, small flippers, and hardly any beak at all.

The Pacific white-sided dolphin has a black back, gray sides and a white belly, and grows to about 7 feet (2.3 m). It lives in the temperate waters of the North Pacific, where it hunts for hake, sardines, and squid.

▶ *Common dolphin*

▼ *Pacific white-sided dolphin*

Bottlenose dolphin

This dolphin's short, stout beak creases where it meets the forehead, making a shape like the neck of a bottle. It has a long, strong body with relatively short flippers, and *flukes* (the two triangular parts of the tail). It is the largest of the beaked dolphins and can grow up to 13 feet (4.3 m) long. The bottlenose dolphin is usually dark gray on the back, lighter gray on the sides and pinkish white on the belly. Some bottlenose dolphins, however, can be pinkish brown all over.

▲ *Bottlenose dolphin*

Bottlenose dolphins live in temperate and tropical water all over the world. They usually live in coastal waters, but they have also been seen in mid-ocean. They eat a variety of food such as small fish, eels, catfish, mullet, squid, and shrimp. They form good friendships with humans, as you will see when you read the story of Percy and the Monkey Mia dolphins later in this book.

Hourglass dolphin

This dolphin also belongs to the *Lagenorhynchus* group. It differs from others in this group, however, by having a high curved dorsal fin, longer flippers, and a small but distinct beak. Its hourglass shape is created by the striking black and white markings on its stout body. Little is known about this small dolphin, which lives in the cold remote subantarctic and Antarctic waters of the Southern Hemisphere.

Risso's dolphin

The gray grampus or Risso's dolphin has a stout mid-to-dark gray body with a bulbous head and no beak. It can grow up to 13 feet (4.3 m) long. The dorsal fin is tall and sickle-shaped, and the flippers are long.

These dolphins live in tropical or cool temperate waters around the world and are found only in the open ocean. Although they are toothed whales, they have very few teeth. There are none in the upper jaw, and only three to seven on each side of the lower jaw. The roof of the mouth is lined with spiky outgrowths formed of skin. These act almost as "false teeth," and seem to be adequate for their specialized diet of squid and octopus.

Paul Ensor/Hedgehog House, New Zealand

▲ *Hourglass dolphins are very fast swimmers. They seem to skim along the surface of the water.*

▲ *Risso's dolphin*

Commerson's dolphin

This dolphin is easily identified by its stocky black body, the broad snow-white saddle around its trunk, and a white patch beneath its chin. It has no beak, and its flippers and dorsal fin are rounded. Only growing to about 5 feet (1.3 m) long, it is one of the smallest dolphins.

Commerson's dolphins are powerful swimmers and usually travel in small groups. They are found only in a few regions of the cold waters of the Southern Hemisphere, and they eat small fish, squid, and shrimp.

Francisco Erizo/Bruce Coleman Ltd

▲ *Commerson's dolphin looks a little like a harbor porpoise, with its stocky body and no visible beak.*

▶ *Commerson's dolphin*

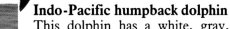

Michael Bryden

▲ *The Indo-Pacific humpback dolphin has a triangular dorsal fin.*

▼ *Hector's dolphin leaps from the water on the coastline of New Zealand.*

Indo-Pacific humpback dolphin

This dolphin has a white, gray, or spotted body with brownish flippers and tail fin, and a light pink belly. Its beak is long and slender, and its dorsal fin is low and triangular. Its flippers are small and rounded.

The dolphins found in the Indian Ocean have a hump on their backs; those found in the Pacific Ocean do not. Small groups of Indo-Pacific humpback dolphins are often seen feeding on reef-dwelling organisms in shallow coastal waters and in estuaries (where fresh water meets the sea).

Hector's dolphin

This is a very beautiful small dolphin. It is only 20 inches (50 cm) at birth, and it can grow up to 6 feet (1.8 m) long. It has a very slight beak, rounded dorsal and pectoral fins, and long, pointed flukes.

Hector's dolphin is found definitely in the waters off New Zealand but there have been unconfirmed sightings from Australia and Borneo. It likes to eat bottom-dwelling fishes, anchovies, crustaceans, and squid.

Steve Dawson/Hedgehog House, New Zealand

Pantropical spotted dolphin

This is an average-sized dolphin that is easily recognized by the dense gray spots that cover its steel-gray body. Its beak is similar in shape to the bottlenose dolphin, but it is more slender and the tip is usually white. The dorsal fin is sickle-shaped, and the flippers are small and pointed.

Pantropical spotted dolphins live in tropical and subtropical regions around the world. They are found in both coastal and deep ocean waters and gather in herds of up to several thousand animals. They are often with spinner dolphins (to which they are closely related) and schools of tuna. They all like to eat the same kinds of fish and squid.

Spinner dolphin

This is the acrobat of the sea — named for its spinning leaps out of the water. It has a slender muscular body with a long narrow beak. Its dorsal fin is tall and triangular and its flippers are long and slender.

◄ *Pantropical spotted dolphin.*

▼ *Spinner dolphin.*

▼ *Spinner dolphins travel the world's major oceans — the Pacific, the Indian, and the Atlantic.*

Marc Webber/Earthviews

Family Phocoenidae

Porpoises are grouped together in the family Phocoenidae, which has six species.

Dall's porpoise

This is the fastest and strongest swimmer of all cetaceans. Traveling at up to 27 knots (30 miles or 50 km per hour) it creates splashes of water spray, which look like rooster's tails, behind it. Its body, which is perfectly designed for moving rapidly in water, is chunky with small flippers, a large streamlined dorsal fin, and a small, rounded head.

Dall's porpoises live in small groups in inshore as well as oceanic waters of the North Pacific. They eat lanternfish, squid, and small schooling fish.

Spectacled porpoise

It does not wear glasses, but it does have two white circles surrounding its eyes. The top half of its body is glossy black, and the belly and lower half of the sides are white. Like all porpoises, the spectacled porpoise has no beak, and its head is small and well rounded. It has a stocky body with short, rounded flippers and a triangular dorsal fin that grows to about 6.5 feet (2 m).

Sightings of spectacled porpoises suggest that they live in the subantarctic waters of the world. They feed on fish and squid.

Harbor porpoise

The harbor or common porpoise has a brown or dark gray back and a light gray belly. It has small rounded flippers, and a blunt dorsal fin. Harbor porpoises swim slowly in pairs or in small groups. They live in cold temperate coastal waters of the Northern Hemisphere and eat a variety of fish, squid, and shrimp.

Finless porpoise

This porpoise has a pale, pinkish gray back and a white belly. Its head is rounded and beakless, and the eyes are often pink. Its flippers are long and slender, and instead of a dorsal fin, there is a low ridge running from the middle of the back to the tail.

Finless porpoises can grow to 6 feet (1.8 m) and are found in warm temperate waters in the Indian Ocean and around southwest Asia. They are coastal animals and are rarely seen more than 3 miles (5 km) from shore. They also move into estuaries, mangrove swamps, and rivers around these shores, but there they risk being killed by fishermen or pollution. Some finless porpoises spend all their lives in China's Yangtze River and never move out to the sea.

▲ *Dall's porpoise is similar in size and shape to Commerson's dolphin.*

▶ *Spectacled porpoise*

▶ *Harbor porpoise*

▶ *Finless porpoise*

Orca, killer whale

The largest dolphin with the most sensational reputation is the orca — or, as it is often called — the killer whale. One film that exploited this reputation was *Orca, the Killer Whale*. In a style similar to the film *Jaws*, it cast the orca as a violent creature that raged through the seas hunting the people who had killed its mate. It smashed boats and houses in a frenzy of destruction. But in contrast to this violent image, trained orcas are actually very gentle with humans. They will let humans ride on their backs, and they are among the "smartest" and easiest to train of all toothed whales. Why do they have such a fearsome name?

Perhaps it is because orcas are efficient killers and eat warm-blooded sea mammals. They feed and hunt cooperatively in stable groups or "pods" of two to fifty orcas. They use a special language of clicks, whistles and pulsed (drumming) calls to communicate with each other and organise themselves for a successful attack. One pod studied in the coastal waters off Argentina, South America, are very skillful at trapping seals. They gather at seal pupping grounds and swim close to shore. Some even go so far as to intentionally strand themselves on the beach. This makes the seals panic and try to escape through the surf. Other pod members are lurking in the waters ready to seize them. The stranded orcas then use their flukes or tail fins to pull themselves back into the water.

Even whales are not safe from pods of orcas. Sometimes orcas "herd" whales into shallow waters, then attack and kill them. Orcas have been known to suffocate a great whale's blowhole so it could not breathe or forcing it to remain underwater until it died.

Orcas are found in all oceans of the world and as many as thirty pods, with as many as 260 members, can be found living together. The "language" of each pod varies but there seem to be basic calls that all pods in the same community can understand.

Jen and Des Bartlett/Bruce Coleman Ltd

How to spot an orca

It would be hard not to spot an orca as it can grow to be as large as 30.5 feet (9.4 m). It has a black back and sides, a white underbelly, and a teardrop-shaped white spot behind and above the eye. Unlike most dolphins, it has no distinct beak. The dorsal fin is much larger in males than in females.

◀ *Orcas often swim stealthily to the shore where seals have gathered by the water's edge. The seals get such a fright when they see the orcas that they panic and jump into the water. But . . . the orcas are waiting for the seals, which they attack and kill.*

More toothed whales

Family Delphinidae and Phocoenidae are two families of toothed whales. Other families include the river dolphins, white whales, and beaked whales.

White whales
The narwhal, belukha, and Irrawaddy dolphins belong to this family. White whales have more flexibility in their bodies than other toothed whales, and they also have a more flexible neck. This allows them to turn their heads slightly and twist their bodies while swimming. They do not have a beak and so the head appears blunt and bulbous. The flippers are rounded and flexible, and the dorsal fin is either short or absent.

Where did you get that tooth?

The narwhal's spiral tusk is actually a well-developed tooth. It erupts from the upper jaw in males and can grow to be as long as 8.5 feet (2.5 m). Many centuries ago, these tusks were sold as genuine unicorn horns. Narwhals are still hunted for their tusks, which are carved and sold for ivory and souvenirs.

Fred Bruemmer

White whales get their name from the belukha, which is ivory or white and is the largest member of the family. It grows up to 16 feet (5 m) long. The narwhal and the Irrawaddy dolphin are blue-gray in color and grow to less than 10 feet (3 m) long.

The narwhal and belukha live in Arctic waters. They use their rounded foreheads to break through ice to make holes through which they can breathe. The narwhal is found in more open water, while the belukha usually prefers shallow waters and even travels a long way up major rivers in summer. Their enemies include humans, who hunt them for food (and tusks in the case of the narwhal), orcas, polar bears, and pollution, which contaminates their waters.

The Irrawaddy dolphin lives in tropical estuaries. While its total population is unknown, scientists think that it is a fairly common species.

Hide and seek

The belukha, or white whale, is a slow-moving species. It is not fast enough to outswim its enemies, the orcas. When orcas are scouring the seas for prey, belukhas will sometimes hide in the heavy slush between ice floes, or in the small alcoves in layers of the pack ice. If the orcas pass close by them, the belukhas will become motionless white forms among the ice slabs. The orcas are often outfoxed.

Pat Morris/Ardea London

▼ *Irrawaddy dolphin*

D. Parer & E. Parer-Cook/Auscape

▲ *Irrawaddy dolphins with a trainer at Marineland Park in Jakarta, Indonesia.*

Beaked whales

Although there are 18 species in this family, most of them are rare. Beaked whales have long bodies, small beaks, dorsal fins, and flippers. Unlike other cetaceans, their flukes do not look as if they are made up of two triangles because they do not have a central tail notch (the middle of the tail where the two parts of the tail meet).

Beaked whales are medium-sized whales, which live in the open ocean. The largest species is Baird's beaked whale. It is also called the giant bottlenose whale. Female beaked whales tend to grow larger than males, and female Baird's beaked whales can grow to be as long as 42 feet (12.8 m). Male beaked whales are often heavily scarred from mating fights.

▼ *Baird's beaked whale*

Beaked whales have very few teeth and live mainly on a diet of squid. Some species, however, eat deepwater fish too. Usually they have one or two pairs of teeth in the lower jaw.

Male strap-toothed whales have very unusual teeth. As you might guess from their name, they have two long strap-like teeth that can grow to about 1 foot (30 cm) long and curve out around the beak. Sometimes, these teeth can prevent the beak from opening fully, so strap-toothed whales have developed a way of sucking squid into their mouths.

▶ *Strap-toothed whale*

James D. Watt/Earthviews

▲ *Beaked whales, such as this dense beaked whale, have slender beaks and few teeth. They like to eat squid and fish.*

22

Did you know?

The "baiji" (meaning white dolphin) is one of the twelve most endangered species of animals in the world. It lives in the Yangtze River where it is threatened by pollution, fishermen, and boat propellers. Scientists are studying ways to save the baiji from complete destruction because there are only 250-300 of them left. If these are killed, the species will be extinct.

▼ *The Chinese river dolphin has a long, thin beak, which is tilted slightly upward. It is a very shy dolphin, and its low triangular dorsal fin is often all that is seen of it in the water.*

Nick Gordon/Ardea London

River dolphins

There are four species of river dolphin, and these fall into three separate families. Although its appearance is similar to the river dolphins, the pale brown franciscana belongs in a family of its own. It lives in the ocean, not in rivers.

River dolphins have small, stocky, pale-colored bodies. They grow to only about 9 feet (3 m) long. They have very long, thin beaks, rounded paddle-shaped flippers, and a triangular dorsal fin (if one is present at all). The Ganges River dolphin is mainly gray, the Amazon River dolphin is either pink or pink and gray, and the Chinese river dolphin is gray and white.

River dolphins eat bottom-dwelling fish, such as catfish and shrimp. They use their *echolocation* (a system that enables them to hunt and navigate by sound) to find the fish in the muddy waters. Their eyes are small, and the Ganges River dolphin is almost blind.

River dolphins are threatened by humans. Activities such as damming, river boat traffic, pollution, fishing lines and nets, and hunting for sport and food, have depleted their numbers. The Chinese river dolphin (the baiji), which lives in the Yangtze River, is under great threat. To help its survival, a dolphin sanctuary and scientific research station has been set up at Tongling, a city that has adopted the baiji as its mascot. There are plans to construct similar reserves in other cities. People are more aware of the dangers the baiji faces, and it is now a protected animal and a national treasure.

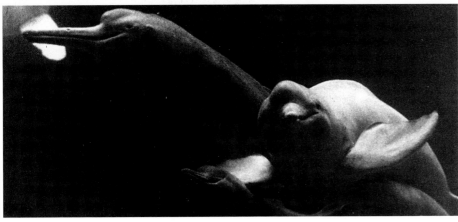

Marineland of Florida

◄ *The bouto or Amazon River dolphin has small but effective eyes. It also has an efficient echolocation system, which it uses to hunt prey in its muddy river home.*

Life in the water

Along with the "great" whales and sea cows, dolphins and porpoises are the only mammals that spend all their lives in the sea. How different is life in the water?

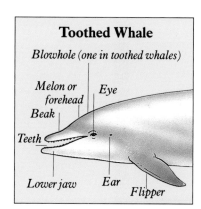

Toothed Whale

Blowhole (one in toothed whales)

Melon or forehead

Eye

Beak

Teeth

Lower jaw

Ear

Flipper

The sea as a home
Water is denser than air. While this makes it harder to move through, it also provides more buoyancy. Animals that live in the water are streamlined in shape as this makes swimming easier.

Look at the shape of any dolphin or porpoise. They resemble a torpedo with their bulbous heads and tapered bodies. They have no sharp edges, and the only parts that stick out are the fins. The flippers and dorsal fins are used for steering and balance, while the powerful tail flukes propel the body through the water. The skin is streamlined too. It is smooth and may discharge oil or mucus to make the body slippery.

Skeletons
The skeleton of dolphins and porpoises is quite different from that of land animals. It is much weaker because dolphins and porpoises do not need limbs to hold them up. The skull is unusual as it is "telescoped" or pushed in from the front to the back and there is a single nostril on top. The bones of the neck are short, the ribs are delicate, and the only remains of a pelvis are two small pieces of bone within the muscles. The forelimbs are well developed into flippers, and there are no back legs.

▼ This bottlenose dolphin has a streamlined body with no rough edges.

Q. How does a dolphin sleep in water without drowning?

A. Scientists believe that when a dolphin sleeps, only half of its brain rests. The other half stays awake to allow the dolphin to function normally. Later the two halves of the brain swap functions.

A cold sea

Heat is transferred more readily in water. That is why people lost overboard at sea — even if they can swim — often die. The heat of their bodies is quickly lost to the colder water. Warm-blooded mammals that make the sea their home need to be able to conserve body heat. They do this in a number of ways.

Firstly, it is an advantage to be large. Whales, seals, dolphins and porpoises are large compared to other (cold-blooded) sea animals. They are able to produce more heat inside their bodies than is lost through the surface of their skin. Secondly, they have a thick layer of fat under the skin, called blubber. This insulates the body and helps to keep the body heat in.

The blood system of aquatic mammals is also made for saving heat. Like humans, dolphins' blood cools down as it flows to the ends of their bodies. Blood vessels in the tail, flippers, and fin are arranged so that the blood flowing back from them is re-warmed before it returns to other parts of the body.

Falcate *Triangular* *Rounded*

Dolphins can have different shaped dorsal fins. They may be falcate (hooked or curved), triangular, or bluntly rounded, such as the fin of this Hector's dolphin. Some dolphins, however, have no dorsal fin at all.

The Skeleton of a Dusky Dolphin

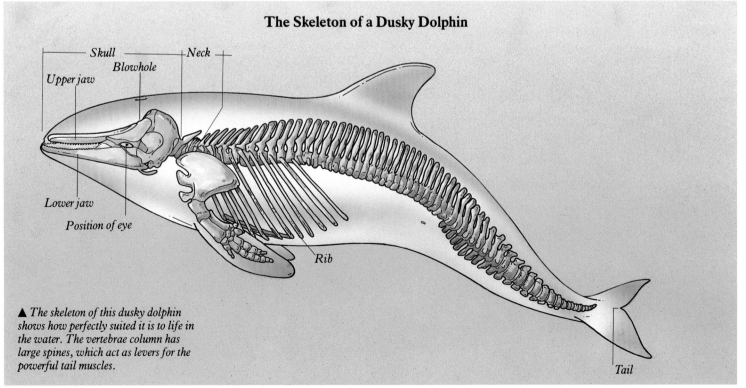

Skull — Neck
Blowhole
Upper jaw
Lower jaw
Position of eye
Rib
Tail

▲ *The skeleton of this dusky dolphin shows how perfectly suited it is to life in the water. The vertebrae column has large spines, which act as levers for the powerful tail muscles.*

Breathing and diving

Whalers have long watched dolphins and porpoises surfacing for air, but until the 1950s little was known about their breathing rates or their dives. By fitting signaling devices on dolphins, scientists have been able to record their whereabouts at all times and make detailed studies in the open ocean. The devices were designed to fall off after a time so that the animal would be unharmed and the equipment could be recovered and used once again.

The experiments showed many variations in diving ability among the different species of toothed whales. Bottlenose beaked whales, for example, are impressive divers. They dive deeply — from 1 to 2 miles (2–3.2 km) — and can stay down for nearly two hours. Bottlenose dolphins, on the other hand, spend 15 minutes underwater between breaths, and common dolphins dive for only three minutes at a time.

Since their blowholes are on top of their heads, dolphins and porpoises need to surface only for a short time. They breathe in and out rapidly. Their lungs are not very large, yet they breathe deeply and efficiently. When they are surfacing, their heart beats two to three times faster than when they are diving. This brings more blood to the lungs. As their blood contains more red blood cells than the blood of other mammals, more oxygen is taken into the body with each breath. Their muscles are also made to store large amounts of oxygen for a short time.

When they dive, dolphins and porpoises hold their breath. Their heart beat slows down, and much of their blood flows to important organs such as the brain and heart muscle. Organs such as the stomach and kidneys do not require much oxygen when the animal is diving. The length of time dolphins and porpoises can spend underwater gives us an idea of their oxygen storage and blood circulation efficiency.

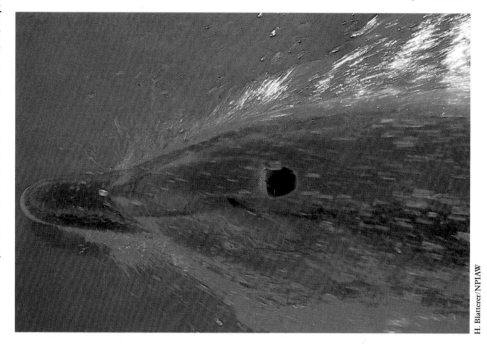

▼ *Dolpins and porpoises breathe air in and out quickly through their blowholes as they surface. When they dive again, their blowholes instinctively close over.*

H. Blatterer/NPIAW

Robert Pitman/Earthviews

▲ *Striped dolphins take very short dives, unlike bottlenose dolphins, which spend nearly 15 minutes underwater between breaths.*

Did you know?

Orcas can raise more than half their bodies straight up out of the water. This is called spy-hopping, and orcas use this to help them hunt for food. While their heads are held well above water they can "spy" all around them — looking for fish, for seals on nearby rocks, beaches or ice floes, or perhaps . . . just looking!

Don Croll

Acrobatics

Swimmers of the Sea

Dolphins and porpoises are very fast swimmers. Some species can reach speeds of 27 miles per hour (45 km or 24 knots)!

In 1948 a scientist called James Grey tried to explain these amazing speeds by carrying out experiments with a dolphin model. He decided that dolphin tail muscles must be ten times more powerful than the muscles of other mammals. This seemed unlikely, but it was not until the early 1960s that another, more logical explanation was given.

Dolphins swim by pushing on the water with their powerful tail flukes. The tail flukes lie horizontally in the water and beat up and down. The upstroke is the power stroke. As the tail is lifted up, it stirs up the water, which makes it rush from above the tail to below it. This makes a whirlpool effect (or *vortex*). The pressure changes that are caused by this effect make the water flow from under the head, up, and over the body. The flippers provide balance, and the animal is pushed forward. The whirlpool is left behind.

The downward stroke does not push the animal forward. The blades of the flukes curl upward, and water spills sideways rather than to the rear. The power stroke is then repeated.

The action of the tail alone, however, is not enough to explain the high speeds that dolphins and porpoises can achieve. Their streamlined bodies and bulbous foreheads also help to reduce "drag" or resistance of the water. But it is their soft skin that really allows them to overcome the resistance of the water to motion.

Dolphins and porpoises use their highly sensitive skin to check pressure changes. They constantly adjust their body shape to prevent any interruption to the flow of water over their bodies. This allows them to swim efficiently at high speeds. Leaping clear of the water reduces drag too!

▶ *Dusky dolphins swimming the open ocean.*

How a dolphin swims

Vortex forms here

▲ *The flukes beat up and down in the water. The upstroke is the power stroke. It stirs up the water, which creates a whirlpool effect (or vortex).*

Area of low pressure

▲ *The water flows from under the head, up, and over the body.*

Vortex is washed away

▲ *The animal is pushed forward and the vortex is left behind.*

D. Parer & E. Parer-Cook/Auscape

Robert Pitman/Earthviews

Did you know?

The bulbous bow of large ships helps reduce drag as they plow through the water. The bulbous or rounded forehead of some fast-swimming whales, such as this pilot whale, seems to work in the same way. It helps them speed along in the water — just like a torpedo!

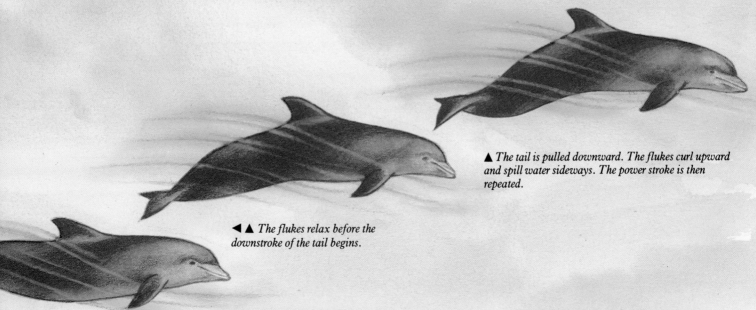

▲ *The tail is pulled downward. The flukes curl upward and spill water sideways. The power stroke is then repeated.*

◄ ▲ *The flukes relax before the downstroke of the tail begins.*

Seeing and sensing

Dolphins and porpoises, like all living creatures, have adapted to their environment. As they live in water but breathe air, their sense organs have adapted to this double life.

As the ancestors of dolphins and porpoises once lived on land, their senses are like ours. However, if we swim underwater we find it hard to see and hear, and we certainly would not try to smell.

Sight
If we try to see underwater everything looks out of focus. To correct this, we wear goggles with flat glass surfaces to trap air around our eyes and keep the water out.

Dolphins and porpoises can focus in both air and water because they have strong eye muscles that change the lens shape. These muscles either contract and make the lens of the eye more rounded for focusing in water, or they relax and the lens becomes more flattened for seeing clearly in air.

When looking at things, either underwater or at the water's surface, dolphins and porpoises often turn on their sides. In this position they use a single eye, which they can move

▼ *This belukha can adjust its eyes to see clearly in both air and water.*

Fred Bruemmer

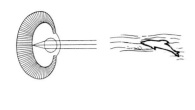

▲ *This diagram shows what happens to light rays when a human and a dolphin try to see in water. A human becomes long-sighted and everything is out of focus. A dolphin, however, is able to focus clearly because it has strong eye muscles that change the lens shape to receive the different light rays.*

▼ *These common dolphins travel in very large numbers. Their well-developed senses enable them to herd and hunt prey successfully.*

Robert Morris

Did you know?

Dolphins and porpoises use their lower jaws in the same way we use our fingers. Scientists believe that this extra sense in the lower jaw helps dolphins and porpoises investigate an object's texture and structure.

around to give a wide range of vision. They can also use both their eyes to focus on things close to them.

Studies with dolphins show they can also recognize some colors, and can change the shape of their pupil to adjust to changes in light and dark as they swim about.

Although light is bright at the water's surface, it is absorbed very quickly with depth. The sea is pitch black at about 200 yards (185 m). Colors also disappear as the water gets deeper. In shallow water all colors can be seen, but the deeper the water, the more blue-green everything appears.

Touch

Dolphins and porpoises have very sensitive skin. It is easily damaged, but it also heals very quickly.

Some skin areas are more sensitive than others. For example, dolphins' mouths and lower jaws are so sensitive they use them the way we use our hands to feel an object.

As the skin of dolphins and porpoises is soft and changes shape easily, it helps them to streamline their bodies and allows them to

Don Croll

swim faster. Scientists also believe that their skin is sensitive to pressure changes which might mean that they can tell whether they are swimming fast or slowly.

Taste and smell

Dolphins and porpoises have a very poor sense of taste, and no sense of smell. This is in stark contrast to sharks, the most successful hunters in the sea.

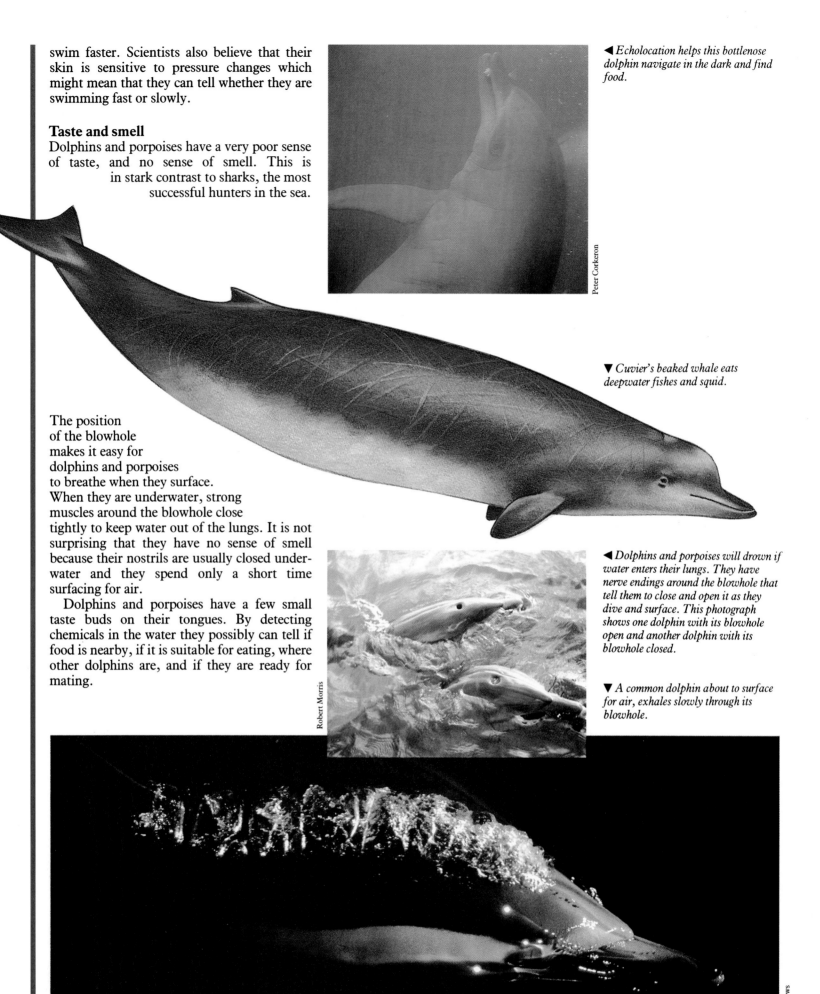

◀ *Echolocation helps this bottlenose dolphin navigate in the dark and find food.*

Peter Corkeron

▼ *Cuvier's beaked whale eats deepwater fishes and squid.*

The position of the blowhole makes it easy for dolphins and porpoises to breathe when they surface. When they are underwater, strong muscles around the blowhole close tightly to keep water out of the lungs. It is not surprising that they have no sense of smell because their nostrils are usually closed underwater and they spend only a short time surfacing for air.

Dolphins and porpoises have a few small taste buds on their tongues. By detecting chemicals in the water they possibly can tell if food is nearby, if it is suitable for eating, where other dolphins are, and if they are ready for mating.

◀ *Dolphins and porpoises will drown if water enters their lungs. They have nerve endings around the blowhole that tell them to close and open it as they dive and surface. This photograph shows one dolphin with its blowhole open and another dolphin with its blowhole closed.*

▼ *A common dolphin about to surface for air, exhales slowly through its blowhole.*

Robert Morris

Ken Balcomb/Earthviews

Hearing and echolocation

Sound is an important sense to dolphins and porpoises. But, because they need streamlined bodies to help them move quickly through the water, they have no external ears. In fact, all we can see of their ears are tiny holes behind each eye.

Dolphins and porpoises have developed a sense that humans and most other land animals are without. It is called echolocation. This means they "see" with sound. Echolocation helps dolphins and porpoises to compete with sharks for food because it allows them to navigate in the dark and find objects that are well out of sight.

Magnetic sense

Another skill or "sense" dolphins and porpoises are believed to have is the ability to "read" the earth's magnetic field and navigate by it.

Sometimes they may make a mistake reading this field. They lose their way and may strand themselves on beaches.

◄ *Pilot whales and certain other species sometimes strand if they make a mistake "reading" the earth's magnetic field.*

Did you know?

Bottlenose dolphins are the dolphins most studied in captivity and in the wild. They live near the coast and are often visible from the shore. If you are lucky enough to have a close encounter with a bottlenose dolphin, remember that its skin is very delicate. It likes to be stroked on the side or on the belly. It does not like to be patted on the "melon" or the forehead.

33

Echolocation

Dolphins and porpoises have their noses on top of their heads, because this position best suits their life in water. The bones of the skull are pushed backward and up over the eye sockets, and extend across the front of the brain area. Scientists think this "telescoping" of the skull bones and extension of the upper jaw is part of the echolocation system.

The echolocation organ in dolphins and porpoises is found inside their heads. An important part of it resembles a melon at the front of the skull. Another part can be seen between the thin jaw bone and ear opening. Both contain fat deposits that are unique because they are made of different substances from ordinary body fat, which is used to store energy.

How a dolphin echolocates

The dolphin makes a series of clicking sounds. These are a mixture of low - and high-frequency clicks. The low-frequency clicks allow dolphins and porpoises to locate and identify objects that are well out of sight. High-frequency clicks — so close together that they make a creaking sound — help them gather information at close range, for example, the size and type of nearby fish.

At an even closer range, they make very high-frequency clicks and touch the object with their lower jaw.

These clicking vibrations travel through the water and bounce off the solid objects, and an echo is reflected back to the animal. The fat deposits in the lower jaw send the vibrations of the echo to the middle ear and highly developed brain. The information is processed here and tells the animal a lot about its environment.

▲ *Scientists think that dolphins may "talk" to one another by whistling sounds.*

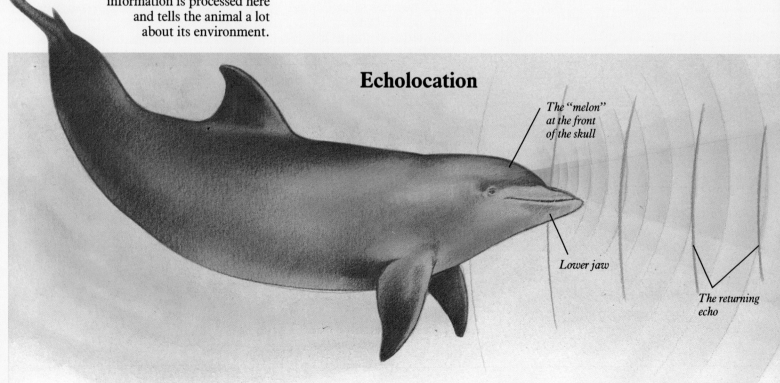

Echolocation

The "melon" at the front of the skull

Lower jaw

The returning echo

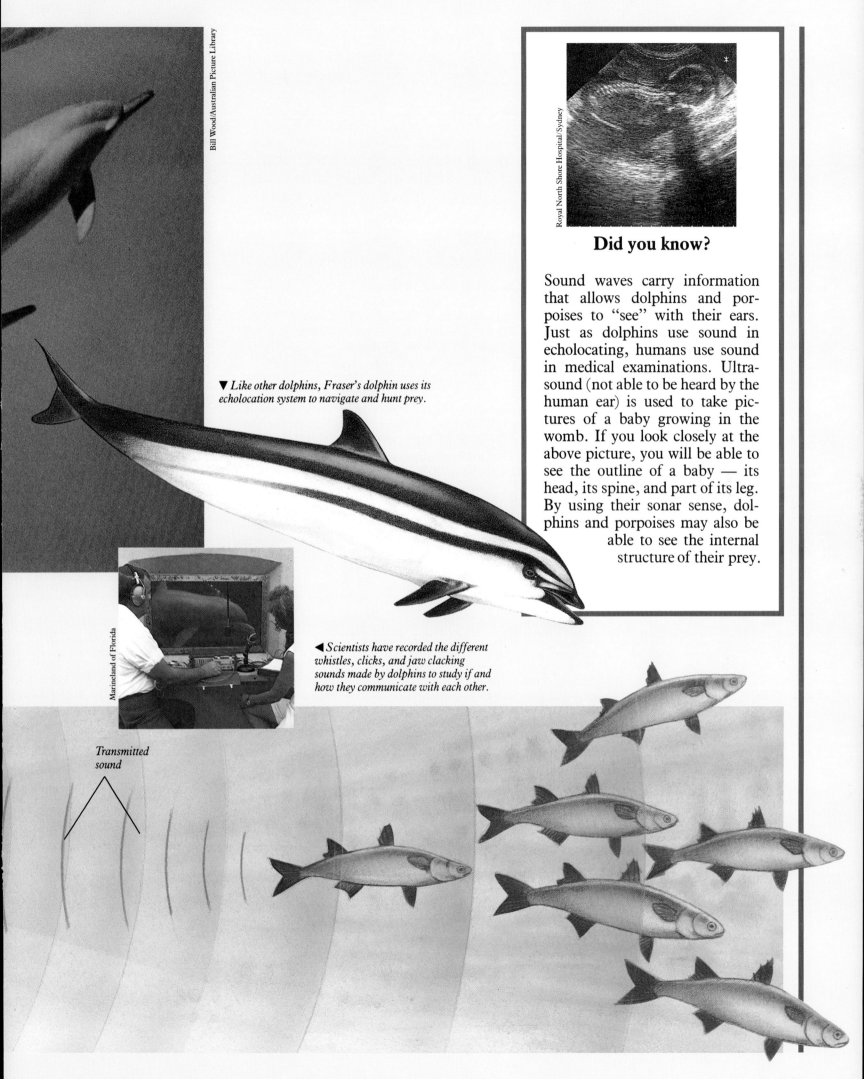

Did you know?

Sound waves carry information that allows dolphins and porpoises to "see" with their ears. Just as dolphins use sound in echolocating, humans use sound in medical examinations. Ultrasound (not able to be heard by the human ear) is used to take pictures of a baby growing in the womb. If you look closely at the above picture, you will be able to see the outline of a baby — its head, its spine, and part of its leg. By using their sonar sense, dolphins and porpoises may also be able to see the internal structure of their prey.

▼ Like other dolphins, Fraser's dolphin uses its echolocation system to navigate and hunt prey.

◄ Scientists have recorded the different whistles, clicks, and jaw clacking sounds made by dolphins to study if and how they communicate with each other.

Transmitted sound

Are dolphins and porpoises intelligent?

When we see dolphins or porpoises in captivity leaping through hoops, responding to signals from a trainer, picking up different shaped objects, and "talking" to each other with clicking sounds and whistles, we think they are intelligent creatures. But intelligence is difficult to study in humans, and even more difficult to measure in dolphins and porpoises.

▲ *Learning to jump through a fiery hoop shows great trust in the trainer rather than being evidence of intelligence.*

What is intelligence?

Intelligence means how much we can understand and reason, and to what extent we are able to adapt to different circumstances. Mimicry, being able to "copy" a skill or behavior, however, should not be confused with intelligence.

Animals such as parrots, pigeons and seals can be taught very complicated tricks yet we do not assume that this means they are understanding and reasoning. We must interpret the "tricks" performed by dolphins and porpoises in the same way.

Brain size and shape

One way scientists have tried to measure intelligence is by brain size. Although the brain of most cetaceans is about the size of the human brain, it is much less developed, particularly in the part that controls body functions and learning.

This part is called the cerebral cortex, and it is much thinner than and different in shape from the human brain. It looks more like the brains of hoofed animals such as cattle, sheep, and deer.

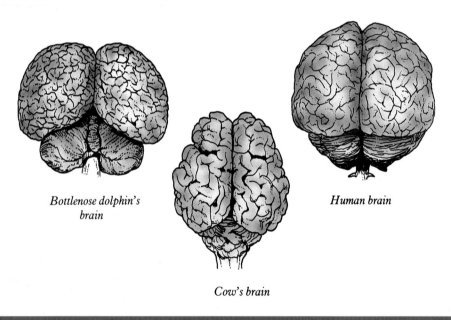

Bottlenose dolphin's brain

Cow's brain

Human brain

Q. If a bottlenose dolphin's brain weighs almost as much as a human brain, does that mean it is as intelligent as a human being?

A. No, say most scientists. Brain size in cetaceans does not mean the same thing as brain size in land mammals, such as apes and humans. Working out the level of intelligence is far more complicated than the size of the brain, although brain size may be a factor.

▲ *False killer whales adapt well to captivity. This false killer whale is showing how it can jump to a height of 24 feet (7.5 m).*

Word play

Studies have been done on dolphins in captivity and in the wild. In captivity dolphins can be taught the difference between certain words and sentence constructions. In one study, balls, pipes, frisbees, and hoops were placed in a dolphin's pool. The dolphins were taught to associate a certain sound or movement with each object. They then learned some verbs, such as "touch" and "feel." When the dolphins were given simple commands, for example, "touch the ball with your tail," they understood and followed the command.

In another study, a bottlenose dolphin was taught to attack sharks that did not usually attack dolphins in the wild, for example, sandbar sharks, lemon sharks, and nurse sharks. But, this dolphin refused to attack a bull shark, which *does* attack dolphins in the wild. This suggests that bottlenose dolphins can tell which sharks are a threat to them.

In the wild, dolphins appear to do intelligent things such as driving fish onto mud banks, then temporarily stranding themselves to eat the fish. They have also been known to help fishermen herd their catch and then share in the take.

But, on the other hand, scientists say dolphins also do very unintelligent things, for example, some dolphins have been unable to free themselves when caught in a net that had many escape routes.

Does this mean some dolphins are more intelligent than others? Possibly, scientists say. However, they also point out that animals such as birds and lions also trick other animals into being caught, and, again, we do not assume they are as intelligent as us.

Studies suggest that sea lions may be more intelligent in certain ways than dolphins. When selecting shapes, a dolphin was found to be less accurate than a sea lion.

Dolphin language

Dolphins make many different sounds such as clicking, whistling, and drumming. The clicking sounds are believed to be part of their highly developed sonar system (echolocation), which they use to "see" objects around them and to navigate. The whistle sounds may be part of a language dolphins use to "talk" to each other, but this theory is still being researched.

▼ *Orcas seem to be intelligent in the way they hunt other animals such as penguins and sea lions.*

▲ *Akeakamai, a bottlenose dolphin, obeys the command "get a hoop and carry it to the pipe."*

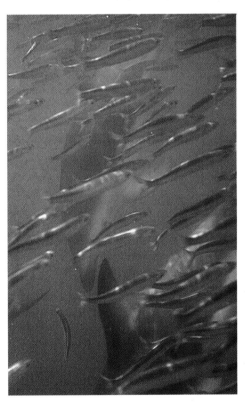

To catch a fish

Certain species of dolphins sometimes herd fish together, close to the shore. The dolphins then rush at the fish, which sets up a small wave that washes the fish ashore. Then, the dolphins deliberately strand themselves to eat the fish that are also stranded on the shore.

Birth and growing up

We do not know much about reproduction and development in the various species of dolphins and porpoises. What we do know has come from research on animals that have either died accidentally or have been hunted and killed intentionally. The only studies of live animals are those carried out on dolphins and porpoises kept in captivity.

Male or female?

It is not easy to tell male and female cetaceans apart. In some species, males are larger than females, but otherwise both sexes look alike. Male orcas, however, are much larger than females and have a taller, more triangular-shaped dorsal fin. As dolphins' and porpoises' bodies must be streamlined, the genital or sex organs are tucked away inside their bodies.

▼ *Usually it is difficult to tell male and female dolphins apart. Male orcas, however, are larger than female orcas and have a more obvious dorsal fin.*

It is only when you closely examine the belly or underside of a dolphin or porpoise that you can observe any sexual differences. Both males and females have a genital and an anal slit, but in males these slits are much farther apart than in females. Females also have two small mammary (milk) slits on either side of their genital slit. The nipples stick out of these slits only when mother dolphins are suckling their young.

The internal sex organs of dolphins and porpoises are similar to other mammals.

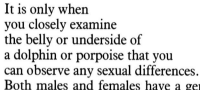

Hitching a ride!

Baby finless porpoises often ride on their mother's back. They are able to do this because the finless porpoise does not have a dorsal fin. Instead it has a long, narrow edge extending down the back from the flippers to near the flukes.

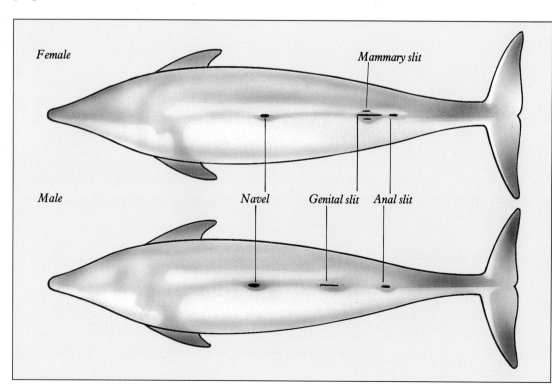

Female — Mammary slit

Male — Navel — Genital slit — Anal slit

Sex organs

The male's penis is made of tough, fibrous tissue. It is held inside the body by two strong muscles. The testes (testicles) lie just behind the kidneys.

The female sex organs are similar to most female mammals. The vaginal wall has many folds that point towards the womb. They may stop water from reaching the womb where the calf grows. The two ovaries are found behind the kidneys.

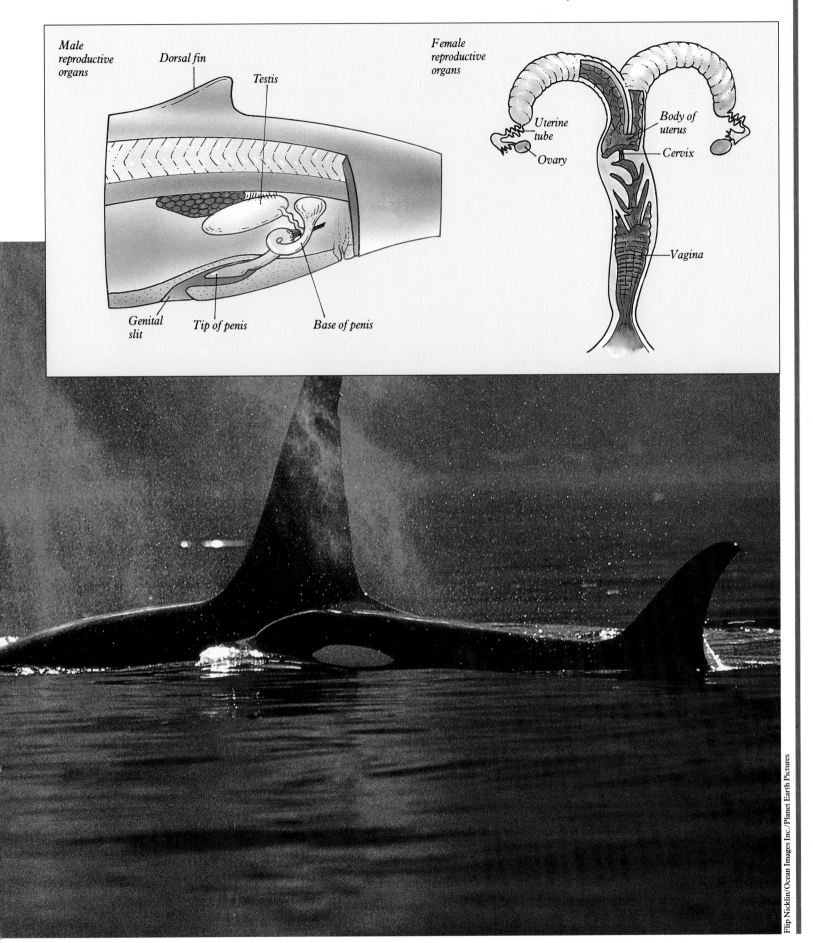

Male reproductive organs

Dorsal fin

Testis

Genital slit

Tip of penis

Base of penis

Female reproductive organs

Uterine tube

Ovary

Body of uterus

Cervix

Vagina

Flip Nicklin/Ocean Images Inc./Planet Earth Pictures

Courtship and mating

Because dolphins and porpoises have no sense of smell, so they must rely on behavioral signals to indicate their willingness to mate. This includes chasing, nuzzling, and rubbing. When mating does occur, the male swims underneath the female and joins with her at right angles to her body.

Giving birth

The young are nurtured inside the female's body, and the pregnancy lasts from nine to eighteen months, depending on the species. Birth occurs underwater, and the usual method of delivery is tail flukes first. In land mammals we call this a breech birth (that is, being born feet first). Sometimes this type of birth can

◀ This Irrawaddy dolphin calf is being born tail first. Mother and calf must then surface quickly so that the calf can take its first breath.

P. Arnantho/Earthviews

Jeff Foott/Survival Anglia

▲ An orca swims with her calf, which was born after thirteen to sixteen months in the mother's womb. It is suckled by the mother for at least a year.

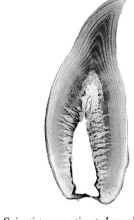

▲ *Scientists can estimate how old a dolphin is by looking at growth layers of teeth. Can you see the different rings in this tooth? This short-finned pilot whale was 29.5 years old.*

▼ *The "spotless" dolphin in this photograph is a young spotted dolphin. Spots develop on its skin as it grows older.*

cause problems. The spindle-like shape of the newborn dolphin or porpoise calf, however, means that it can be born either head or tail first. Multiple births are extremely rare.

The whole birthing process is over very quickly as both the mother and the newborn calf must surface for air. Newborn calves instinctively know not to open their blowhole until they reach the surface. Mothers protect their young and drive off any intruders. They are assisted in this by other females in the same social group, called "aunts".

Calves are suckled underwater but close to the surface so that mother and baby can come up for air from time to time. The milk is squirted straight into the calf's mouth by the mother's muscles. Calves remain close to their mothers for at least a few days or weeks after birth. Suckling continues for more than a year in most species.

Length of life

We do not really know for sure how long dolphins and porpoises live. But by studying growth layers of teeth — much like growth rings in tree trunks — male bottlenose dolphins have been estimated to live for 25 years and females for 30 years. A female bottlenose dolphin, born into captivity 30 years ago, is still alive today. She is even a grandmother!

Did you know?

Newborn dolphins have "aunts". They are dolphins who may help the mother guide the calf to the surface for its first breath, protect it from attack, or support a dead or sick calf at the surface. The many stories of dolphins saving people in the sea may really be cases of mistaken identity. The "rescuing" dolphins may think they are helping a sick calf.

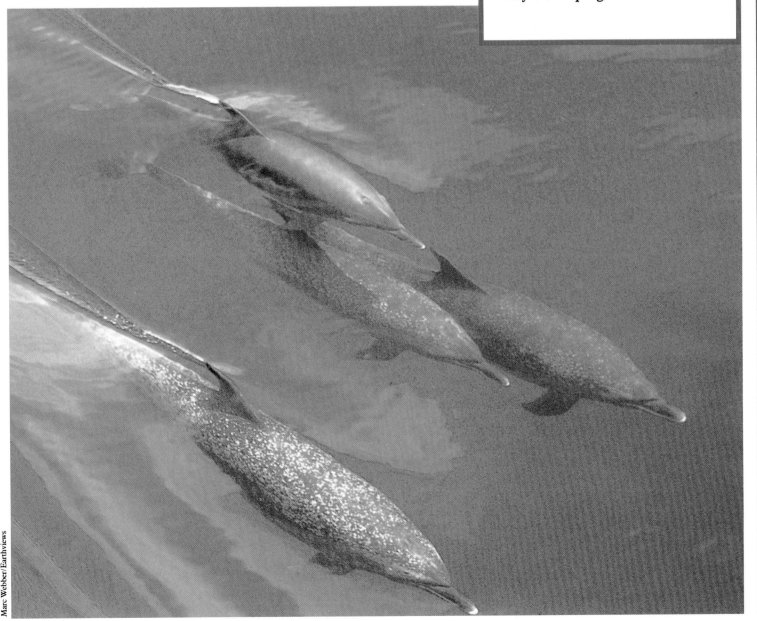

Where do dolphins and porpoises live?

Dolphins and porpoises are found in all oceans of the world and even in some freshwater environments. Each species has different needs and will stay in a particular region or waters that meet these needs.

The ocean may look the same all over to us, but beneath the featureless surface there is another world as varied as our own. There is a wide range of temperatures, salinity (saltiness), light, and currents associated with changes in depth and latitude. The ocean floor itself changes. It may seem flat where it meets the land, but beneath the sea there are towering mountain ranges, vast canyons, and broad plains. These different conditions allow a great variety of organisms to live in the sea.

When describing where aquatic animals are found it is useful to name the areas of the ocean by their latitude. The map on this page shows how this is done. Waters nearest the North Pole are called Arctic (and subarctic) and those nearest the South Pole, Antarctic (and subantarctic). Moving toward the equator from these waters, the areas around the latitudes are cold temperate, warm temperate, subtropical, and finally, tropical.

Generally speaking, the waters are warmer the closer they are to the equator. Depth and currents also influence water temperatures.

▼ *Imagine the problems you would have trying to feed in shallow waters if you had only one enormous tooth, such as these narwhals. That is why they feed only in the deep, open ocean.*

Fred Bruemmer

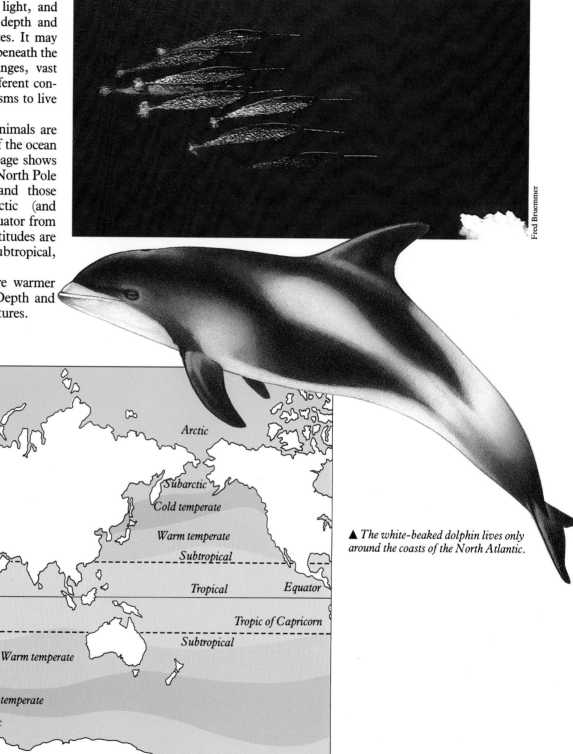

▲ *The white-beaked dolphin lives only around the coasts of the North Atlantic.*

Arctic

Subarctic

Cold temperate

Warm temperate

Subtropical

Tropic of Cancer

Tropical

Equator

Tropic of Capricorn

Subtropical

Warm temperate

Cold temperate

Subantarctic

Antarctic

The *Lagenorhynchus* group is the largest genus in the family Delphinidae. The map on this page shows you where dolphins belonging to this genus are found. As you can see, some, for example, the hourglass dolphin, have a wide distribution. It lives in cold subantarctic and Antarctic waters. Others, for example, the dusky dolphin, live in more restricted areas. The dusky dolphin is found in the temperate coastal waters around most of the continents and around several islands of the Southern Hemisphere.

In the Northern Hemisphere the white-beaked and the Atlantic white-sided dolphins live in the North Atlantic. The Pacific white-sided dolphin lives in the offshore waters of the warm North Pacific.

Porpoises also have varying distributions. The spectacled porpoise lives in small pockets of the ocean from the western South Atlantic to New Zealand waters and subantarctic islands. Dall's porpoise, however, lives in the cold waters of the North Pacific Ocean.

▼ *The spinner dolphin lives in the same tropical waters as its close relative the spotted dolphin.*

Frans Lanting/Bruce Coleman

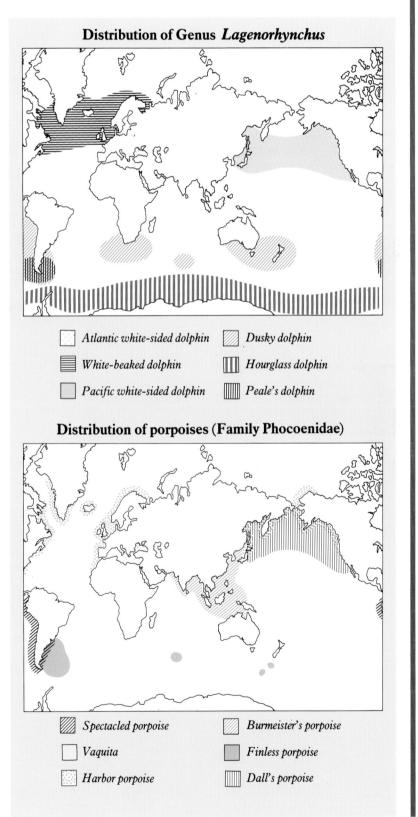

Distribution of Genus *Lagenorhynchus*

Atlantic white-sided dolphin	Dusky dolphin
White-beaked dolphin	Hourglass dolphin
Pacific white-sided dolphin	Peale's dolphin

Distribution of porpoises (Family Phocoenidae)

Spectacled porpoise	Burmeister's porpoise
Vaquita	Finless porpoise
Harbor porpoise	Dall's porpoise

Did you know?

Hector's dolphin is found only in the coastal waters of New Zealand and never more than five miles (8 km) from shore. It is not a shy animal, and it will often approach boats entering New Zealand harbors or follow fishing trawlers. Even though it swims so close to the shore, its small size often makes it difficult to see in rough seas.

Steve Dawson/Hedgehog House, New Zealand

Food for dolphins and porpoises

Nearly all dolphins and porpoises eat squid. Depending on the type of teeth they have and where they live, their diet may also include a variety of fish. The largest dolphin, the orca, also eats seabirds, turtles, sharks, seals, whales, and other dolphins and porpoises.

Teeth types

The ancestors of dolphins, porpoises, and whales had teeth. The "great" whales evolved into toothless creatures, but dolphins and porpoises kept their teeth. Today's dolphins and porpoises differ from their ancestors because they have more teeth, which are all identical. Most have between 20 and 80 teeth in each of the upper and lower jaws.

Dolphin teeth are small, sharp, and pointed, whereas porpoise teeth are small but spade-shaped. There are, however, some interesting exceptions. The rough-toothed dolphin, for example, has wrinkled enamel on its teeth. Risso's dolphin has no teeth at all in the upper jaw and only three to seven teeth on each side of the lower jaw.

Most of the beaked whales have only two teeth, which are both in the lower jaw. The male narwhal — the most unusual toothed whale of them all — has a single tooth that erupts to form a tusk.

▼ *This well-preserved fossil is the skull of a killer whale.*

Jeff Foott/Survival Anglia

Did you know?

Dolphins do not chew their food. Their teeth are not designed to do this. Although they have many more teeth than most mammals, their teeth are all small, sharp, and pointed. They can be used only to grip this slippery fish, which is then swallowed whole.

Ben Cropp

44

Diet

The shape of the dolphin's head, as well as the shape and number of its teeth, indicate what sort of food it eats. Broad-headed dolphins have very few teeth and live almost entirely on squid. Such different species as Risso's dolphin and the beaked whales have the same broad head shape and few teeth because they have evolved eating the same type of food.

Narrow-headed dolphins with many teeth, such as the pantropical spotted dolphin and the spinner dolphin, mainly eat fish. Dolphins and porpoises with "in-between" head and teeth characteristics, however, eat a greater range of food.

▼ *Like the narwhal, the belukha feeds in Arctic waters, but only in shallow waters, bays, and rivers.*

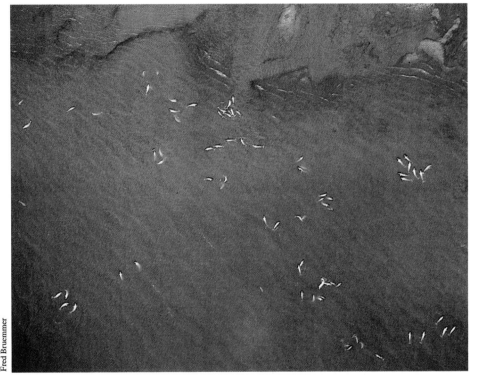

Fred Bruemmer

Feeding behavior

What dolphins and porpoises eat also influences their social behavior. Dolphins and porpoises feed and live independently or in pairs when their food is evenly spread and there are places to hide from their enemies. The Indo-Pacific humpback dolphin, which feeds in rocky reef areas, and river dolphins, which probe muddy river bottoms for small fish, follow this behavior pattern.

Dolphins and porpoises living in inshore bays and along ocean beaches usually form small groups of between six and twenty animals. Their food is often clumped together in patches and they are more exposed to danger from predators.

Open-ocean dolphins and porpoises form groups of several hundred animals. Their food is scattered over huge areas, and large groups can herd schools of fish and squid more successfully.

Animals such as spinner dolphins that move between coastal waters and the open ocean, vary their group size. Spinner dolphins can be seen resting alone or swimming slowly in small groups in inshore bays during the day. At night they move offshore in large groups to feed on open-ocean fish.

Sometimes, it is possible to find feeding groups made up of many different kinds of animals. A rich food source out to sea, for example, could bring together such different species as the bottlenose dolphin, Risso's dolphin, the rough-toothed dolphin, the pantropical spotted dolphin, the striped dolphin, the common dolphin, and the false killer whale. A toothed whales party!

▼ *Dolphin and porpoises' teeth vary in shape and size depending on their jaw size and the type of food they eat.*

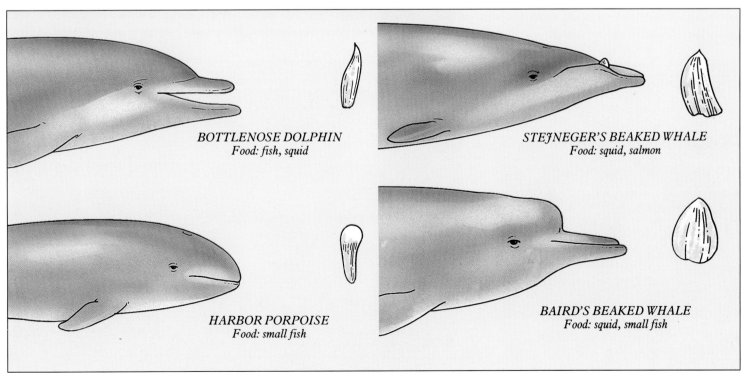

BOTTLENOSE DOLPHIN
Food: fish, squid

STEJNEGER'S BEAKED WHALE
Food: squid, salmon

HARBOR PORPOISE
Food: small fish

BAIRD'S BEAKED WHALE
Food: squid, small fish

Tuna netting

Dolphins and porpoises eat the same food as yellowfin and skipjack tuna. Tuna fishermen set their nets around dolphins, knowing that tuna will be caught at the same time. In the 1950s, the United States established a successful tuna fishing industry by exploiting this link between dolphins and tuna.

Tuna catching involves setting nets in areas where dolphins are seen. The nets, called *purse-seines*, are huge and can be three-quarters of a mile (1 km) long and 140 yards (130 m) deep. (Imagine an area more than 10 football fields long and one football field deep.) The main vessel casts a net, and speedboats chase the dolphins, rounding them up so that the net can easily encircle them. The bottom of the net is drawn together, and the whole net is then pulled in. The tuna, which are close by the dolphins, also get caught.

While this method is very successful for catching tuna, it has also meant the death of a large number of dolphins. Between 1959 and 1972, an estimated 4.8 million dolphins were killed this way by registered fishing vessels alone. The real death count is probably much greater.

The United States National Marine Fisheries Service (NMFS) carried out research to try to prevent so many dolphin deaths, while still allowing the tuna fishing industry to thrive. Their suggestions included redesigning portions of the seine nets and the way they are pulled in, which would allow dolphins to escape, and also releasing trapped dolphins "by hand." In areas where tuna netting has been carried out for many years, some dolphins have learned to flee from the nets, or when caught, to wait calmly to be released by the crew.

Quotas or limits were also introduced. The United States government allows 20,000 dolphins a year to be killed *incidentally* before tuna fishing must stop. The Inter-American Tropical Tuna Commission (IATTC) estimates that 55,000 dolphins were killed in 1985, and between 125,000 and 129,000 in 1986.

Unfortunately, other countries have successful tuna netting operations but do not set quotas on dolphin catches. So far, there seems to be little hope for an international solution to the problem.

Did you know?

Dolphins have changed their behavior around fishing boats. In waters where fishing has been carried out for many years, dolphins now swim away from boats that approach them. Some have also learned to flee from the nets. If they do become trapped by nets, many dolphins, such as this one, have learned to wait calmly to be released by the crew.

P.S. Hammond

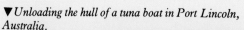
▼ *Unloading the hull of a tuna boat in Port Lincoln, Australia.*

Gunther Deichmann/Auscape

▲ *Herds of spotted dolphins often feed with tuna. This means they are often caught with the tuna in the nets.*

Robert Pitman/Earthviews

▲ *Hundreds of thousands of spotted dolphins have been killed by tuna netting operations.*

▶ *These enormous purse-seine nets stretch out across the sea to catch tuna.*

Stories from the sea

Jean-Luc Bozzoli/Ocean Bozzoli Productions

Much has been written about the mystical connection between humans and dolphins. The earliest examples of this bond come from Greek and Roman drawings and poetry. People of ancient times believed dolphins had special powers because they came from the ocean — the source of all life. Many people today still believe this.

▲ *Even today artists are fascinated by dolphins and their seemingly mystical powers. This painting is by French artist Jean-Luc Bozzoli.*

Ancient art

One day you may visit the island of Crete in the Mediterranean Sea. Perhaps you have been there already. Knossos was once the capital of the Minoan civilization, which ruled Crete from 3000 to 1100 B.C. In the ruins of the Palace of Knossos, you can see some of the earliest wall paintings of dolphins. These frescoes were painted in the period 1450–1400 B.C. (more than 3,000 years ago), and they are very detailed and beautiful. Dolphins were also supposed to be lucky for travelers, and so they were pictured on ancient Roman coins (like the St Christopher Medallion today).

The Dionysus Cup (540 B.C.), a famous piece of Greek art, tells the story of Dionysus, the Greek god of wine and drama. Dionysus saves himself from his crew, who plotted to sell him into slavery, by turning their oars into snakes. The terrified sailors jump into the sea to escape from the snakes. They are saved by the sea god Poseidon, who turns them into dolphins. To thank him for saving their lives, they draw his sea chariot and obey his commands.

Dolphin stories

One of the most powerful gods in Greek mythology was Apollo, the sun god. He fought and defeated Delphyne, the dolphin/womb monster. To celebrate his victory, Apollo turned himself into a dolphin and ruled the universe. Apollo named the Greek city of Delphi (Dolphin Town) after the battle with Delphyne, and built a temple there.

Today in Delphi, central Greece, the remains of this temple, which has been rebuilt a number of times, can still be seen.

Aristotle, a famous Greek philosopher and writer (384–322 B.C.), wrote many stories that have been passed down by word of mouth from generation to generation. Today we can read the stories Aristotle recorded about gentle dolphins allowing children to play with them and ride on their backs through the ocean.

Pliny the Elder, a famous writer from Roman times (about A.D. 23–79), wrote a story of a young boy and a dolphin called Simo. The boy lived in Hippo, a small town on the coast of Tunisia, North Africa. He became friends with a dolphin after it saved him from drowning. The two would play together, and people in the town began watching the two friends. As the story of this unusual friendship spread throughout the country, many people started coming to the town. Merchants soon realized that they could make money renting rooms and selling food. Unfortunately, with so many tourists visiting the town, food, water, and housing became scarce.

People started to fight and quarrel among themselves and eventually the town elders decided something had to be done. They killed the dolphin.

With the coming of Christianity, Greek and Roman mythology was adapted by the church leaders. Dolphins that once helped pagan gods now saved Christian saints from being killed. Early Christian art showed the dolphin as a symbol of love, diligence, and swiftness.

Today some people still seem to regard dolphins as god-like creatures with mysterious powers, just as the early artists and writers did more than two thousand years ago.

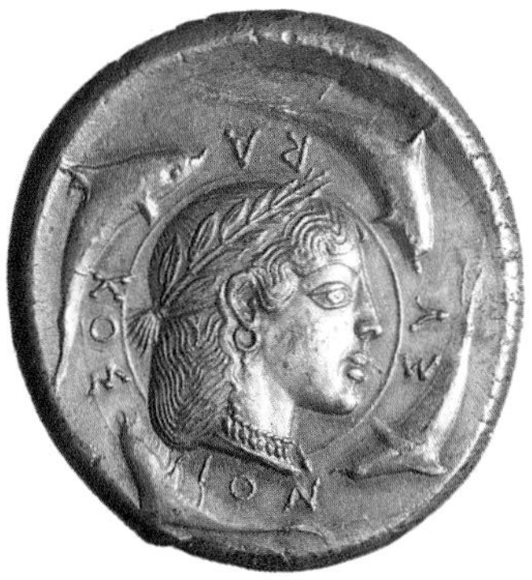

Michael Holford/British Museum (Natural History)

▲ *Dolphins often appeared on ancient coins, as they were considered lucky for travelers.*

▼ *This fresco of dolphins was painted on the wall of the Queen's Room at the Palace of Knossos, Crete, around 1450-1400* B.C.

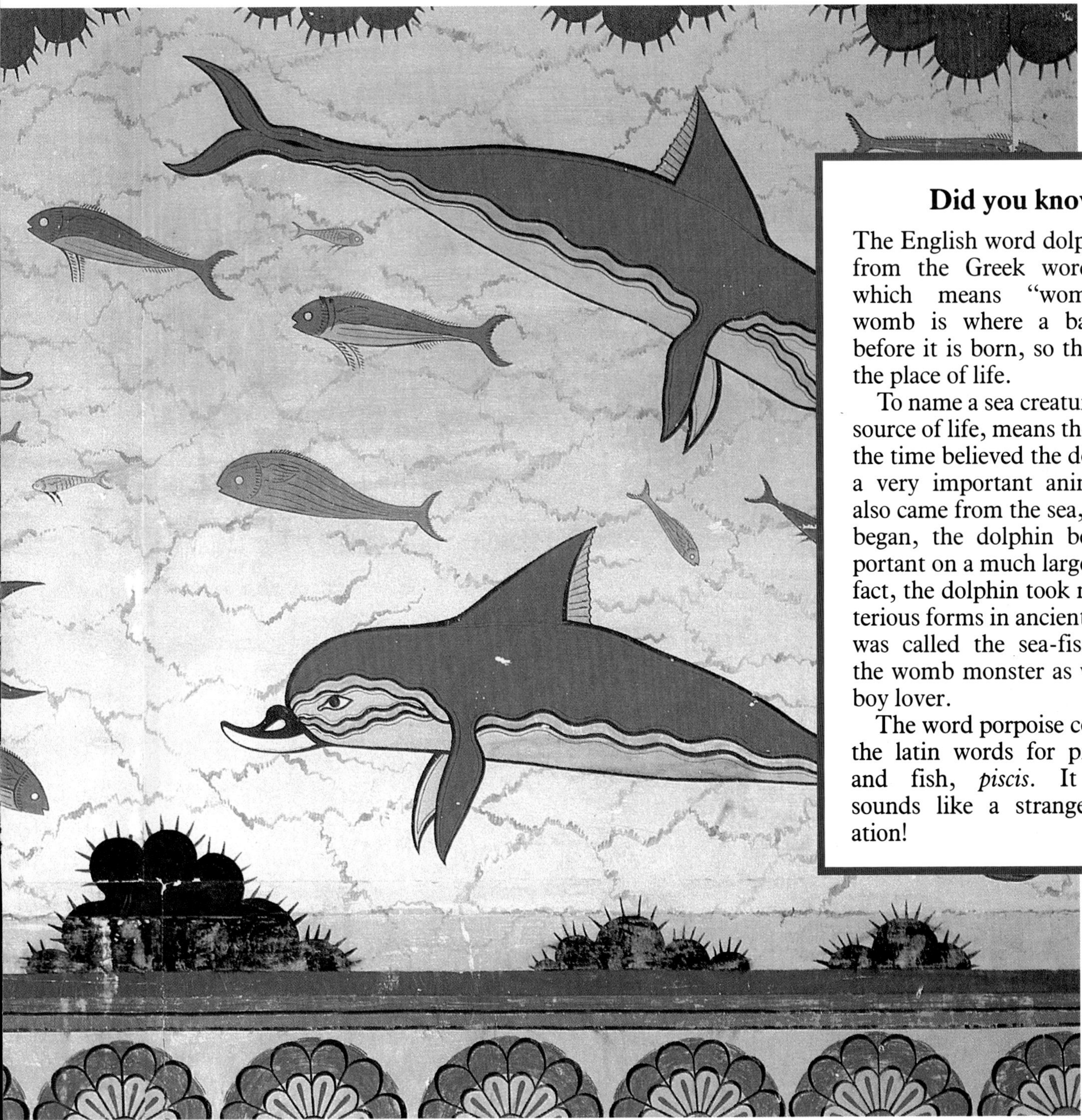

Michael Holford

Did you know?

The English word dolphin comes from the Greek word *Delphis,* which means "womb." The womb is where a baby grows before it is born, so the womb is the place of life.

To name a sea creature after the source of life, means the people of the time believed the dolphin was a very important animal. As it also came from the sea, where life began, the dolphin became important on a much larger scale. In fact, the dolphin took many mysterious forms in ancient stories. It was called the sea-fish mother, the womb monster as well as the boy lover.

The word porpoise comes from the latin words for pig, *porcus,* and fish, *piscis.* It certainly sounds like a strange combination!

Since the Middle Ages, narwhal tusks have been sold as "genuine" unicorn tusks by dishonest traders. The unicorn was a mythical animal, which looked like a horse, apart from having a long, straight horn growing out of its forehead. This horn was thought to have magical powers. It was supposed to be able to detect poison in food or drink, and it was also ground up and used as a potion to cure all kinds of ills. Unfortunately for the narwhals, those beliefs made their tusks highly sought after.

THE NARWHAL OR SEA UNICORN
F. Cuvier

British Museum (Natural History)

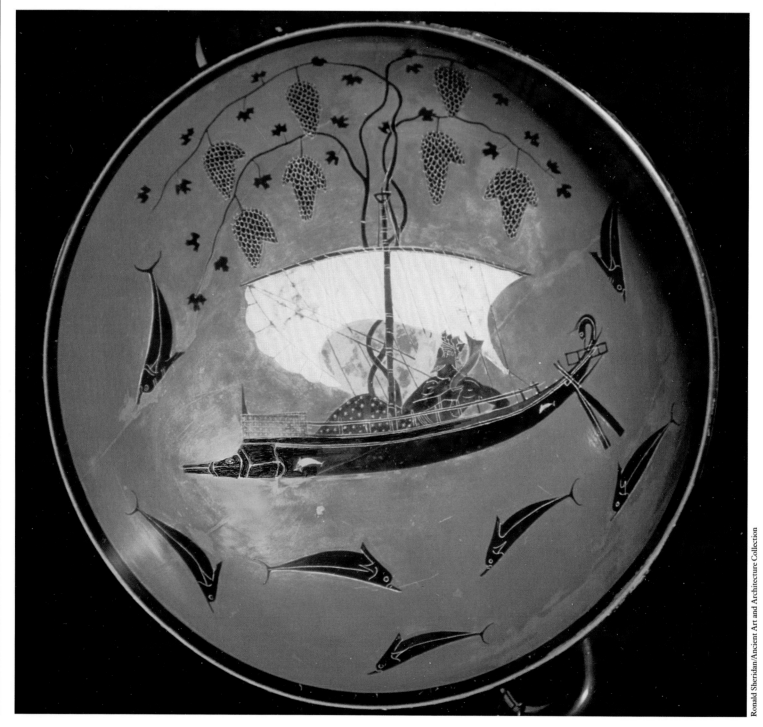

Ronald Sheridan/Ancient Art and Architecture Collection

Dolphins in history

The importance of dolphins to humans has continued through history. The eldest son of the kings of France used to have the title *dauphin*, which is the French word for dolphin. That custom remained for many hundreds of years until the middle of the nineteenth century. Nobody knows where the title came from, but it may have come from an early ruling family from south-eastern France who had a dolphin in its coat of arms.

Since the early 1960s, when the first film starring a dolphin called Flipper was made, we have become much more interested in and knowledgeable about dolphins. *Namu, the killer whale*, a film about an orca, showed this large dolphin's gentleness with humans, and helped audiences to be more aware of these appealing creatures.

◄ *The famous Dionysus Cup tells the story of the Greek god of wine and drama.*

► *A sculpture of the baiji in the Chinese city of Tongling, which has adopted the baiji as its mascot.*

Kaiya Zhou

Aelian: the dolphin of Iassos

This is one of the most famous stories of Greek legend. Nobody really knows if the story of the boy and the dolphin is true. It is believed to have been written at a time when whales and dolphins were known as friends of fishermen and it was considered bad luck to kill them.

One day after running and wrestling at the local gymnasium some of the boys from the Greek town of Iassos went down to the beach to wash. A dolphin swimming nearby

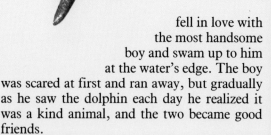

fell in love with the most handsome boy and swam up to him at the water's edge. The boy was scared at first and ran away, but gradually as he saw the dolphin each day he realized it was a kind animal, and the two became good friends.

They spent hours swimming, playing, and diving together, and sometimes the dolphin would let the boy ride on its back like a horse. Each day the dolphin would wait at the shore for the boy to finish school, and they would play in the waves. The townspeople were amazed and loved to watch the boy and the dolphin playing together.

But one day when the boy was very tired, he threw himself down onto the dolphin's back. His navel hit the sharp dorsal fin, which cut him open, and the boy bled to death.

The dolphin did not realize anything was wrong until he felt the boy's body become very heavy, and he noticed the ocean was red with blood. In his sadness the dolphin threw himself and the dead boy onto the beach near the gymnasium where they had first met. There they lay together; the dead boy and the stranded, dying dolphin.

The dolphin's love for the boy so impressed the people of Iassos that they built a monument showing a boy riding on a dolphin. They also made silver and bronze coins, which told the story of their love.

◄ *An ancient bronze statue of the dolphin and boy of Iassos.*

Did you know?

In 1956, a bottle-nose dolphin visited Opononi Beach in New Zealand. "Opo," as the female dolphin became known, made friends with 13-year-old Jill Baker, and would often carry Jill on her back. Opo's fame spread throughout New Zealand and visitors poured into the beach. Everyone wanted to touch Opo — some people would even run fully clothed into the water to do so. When Opo died suddenly, messages of sympathy were sent from all over New Zealand.

The story of Percy

There have been many stories about friendships between dolphins in captivity and their trainers, but there are only a few stories about wild dolphins becoming friendly with humans.

In 1981, off the north coast of Cornwall, England, a dolphin was seen following local boats and divers. He kept his distance until 1983, when he made friends with a diver and spent a lot of time with him.

During that year the diver noticed that the dolphin's behavior had changed and he discovered that Percy (as he named him) had a large fish hook in his head near the right eye. Percy would not let anybody near him during that winter, but by the following spring the hook had disappeared and he became friendly again.

Percy used to follow the local fishing boats when they set their lobster pots and he loved to play with the pots anchored on the ocean floor. Once he got them so tangled the fishermen had to call in a diver to help undo the mess. The diver happened to be Percy's friend, and Percy appeared to help him by pointing to different lines with his jaw to show him how to untie the knots.

Another day when the diver jumped into the water Percy tried to push him back into the boat. When the diver tried to resist, Percy took his hand in his mouth — making him bleed — and pulled him back to the boat. The diver was

very puzzled but later when he returned to the water Percy was friendly again. The only explanation the diver could find was that sharks had been seen in the area and perhaps Percy had been trying to save his friend.

Percy became very friendly and would play with the many people now observing him. He would let them hang onto his dorsal fin and be pulled through the water.

In 1984 he became a celebrity. He was "discovered" by national television and newspapers. One newspaper even published a photograph of Percy apparently "drinking" a cup of tea with some of his admirers. Percy's fame spread and for weeks he was constantly surrounded by people.

With so many people in the water around him, Percy became frightened, and less friendly. He charged at fishing boats, and even jumped at a windsurfer, throwing himself on and breaking the windsurfer's board.

The townspeople started to have arguments about what to do with him and the situation became quite unpleasant. The summer ended, and the tourists left. Percy calmed down and returned to his friendly ways. That winter he disappeared.

▼ *Percy, a bottlenose dolphin, used to "help" the scientists studying him by diving down and picking up the anchor for them.*

Horace E. Dobbs

▲ *Percy helps a diver to find the boat's anchor.*

Horace E. Dobbs

▲ *Percy took food from certain people. Unwelcome visitors were butted or lightly bitten.*

Dolphins, porpoises, and people

People still have a lot to learn about living peacefully not only with each other but also with the creatures that occupy the planet with us. Dolphins and porpoises seem to find us as interesting as we find them, but we threaten their survival by "incidental" killings and pollution.

▲ *Better diving equipment means that skindivers can now study the world of the dolphin more easily.*

▼ *Orcas have occasionally attacked sailing boats but they are more likely to attack other sea creatures.*

There is a lot of evidence to show that dolphins and porpoises like people. They often come up beside boats, swim along with fishing trawlers, and form friendships with divers. The Monkey Mia dolphins of Western Australia have formed a unique contact with the people who visit the area. Dolphins are also show-offs and love to demonstrate their jumping skills when they know humans are watching.

There are many reports of dolphins co-operating with humans. The Atlantic humpback dolphin, which lives in the waters off the west coast of Africa, is said to herd fish into nets at the shore when it hears the fishermen slap the water with sticks. It then shares the catch with the fishermen.

Bottlenose dolphins perform simple tasks and enjoy play with humans. There have

A helping hand

Orcas sometimes helped whalers of old by herding whales into a bay and keeping them on the surface so the whalers could easily catch and kill them. Dolphins have also been known to drive snapper (a fish they do not eat) into shore for fishermen.

▲ *The dorsal fin of this dolphin was slashed by a boat propeller.*

KILLER WHALE RESERVE
STAY 300 METRES
AWAY FROM WHALES

▲ *Natural reserves protect the animals and help scientists to study them in their natural environment.*

also been reports of dolphins saving people from drowning by bringing the victims to the surface and pushing them to safety in shallow water.

Unfortunately for dolphins, not all contact with humans is friendly. Each year thousands of dolphins are killed in tuna nets, and many are killed for food by fishermen. The fishermen also kill dolphins because they see them as competitors for the fish they are trying to catch. By 1974, the Japanese population of striped dolphins had been reduced to half its original 400,000.

River dolphins are under the greatest threat because of pollution, the building of dams, and increased boat traffic on the waterways.

Despite international laws protecting dolphins and porpoises from slaughter, thousands of black dolphins and Burmeister's porpoises are killed each year off the coast of Chile for crab bait.

Although measures are being taken to protect dolphins and porpoises, they still have to deal with human-made hazards that are threatening their environments. Oceans continue to be used as dumping grounds for pollutants and many animals studied in recent years have been found to contain a high level of mercury, a poisonous heavy metal, which eventually kills them. If we are not more careful, the only dolphins and porpoises remaining will be those in captivity.

Q. Which dolphin is considered the most friendly to humans?

A. Bottlenose dolphins because they seem to seek out human contact more than any other dolphins. They are very playful and always seem to have a "smile" on their faces. They are favorites with people who visit oceanariums and scientists who study them.

Monkey Mia Dolphins

In an isolated part of the Western Australian coast, at Shark Bay, is a tiny place called Monkey Mia. Until recently Monkey Mia consisted of a trailer park and a fishing jetty. But now, thousands of tourists come every year to experience a rare and special event. They come to meet the wild bottlenose dolphins that have visited the area for more than twenty years.

It all began one hot evening in 1964, when Ninny Watts was trying to find a cool spot to sleep. She was on a boat anchored in the bay, and she kept hearing a dolphin splashing and blowing around the boat. She threw it a fish out of the ice-box.

Gradually the dolphin, which Ninny named Charlie, came to trust her enough to eat out of her hand. Charlie brought other dolphins into Shark Bay, and even after he died his friends continued to visit. These dolphins do not jump through hoops or perform tricks with balls; they are free to come and go as they please.

Scientists say Monkey Mia is unique. In the past, individual dolphins have made friends with one person, but the Monkey Mia dolphins are the only herd of wild dolphins in the world to have made friends with many people.

Every day about twenty dolphins come into the bay and swim up to the jetty. About eight to ten of these swim right to the water's edge to accept the fish tourists feed them.

Before the Western Australian government employed rangers to protect the dolphins, the owners of the trailer park guarded the dolphins and taught people how to treat them. For example, dolphins do not like being patted on the melon-shaped mound on top of their head because it affects their echolocation sense. Humans should not sit on dolphins' backs as their ribs are delicate and break easily. However, dolphins do like to be stroked on their sides or belly, and they love being fed fresh fish.

The Monkey Mia dolphins have occasionally shown humans that they can do things for them in return. They have been known to herd snapper — a fish they never eat, but one that tourists like — into the shallow waters of the bay.

Monkey Mia is a special place because the dolphins come to visit freely. Hopefully the increasing number of tourists who flock there will not hurt the dolphins' environment or drive them away forever.

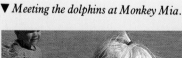

▼ Meeting the dolphins at Monkey Mia.

Hugh Edwards

▲ Wilf and Hazel Mason, the owners of the trailer park at Monkey Mia, looked after the dolphins before rangers were employed to protect them.

Claire Leimbach

◀ *Diver Lyn Cropp feeds fresh fish to a bottlenose dolphin at Monkey Mia. Fish is their favorite snack.*

Did you know?

The bottlenose dolphin is a playful, friendly animal and there are many stories of wild dolphins that have let people play and swim with them. One bottlenose dolphin off the coast of Wales was especially curious and mischievous. It used to let divers swim with it in the open ocean. It would also disrupt diving classes, annoy fishermen, and try to sabotage efforts to film it. Often, it would lift the anchor of a moored boat and with the anchor chain in its mouth, tow the boat away!

▲ *The bottlenose dolphins at Monkey Mia deliberately "strand" themselves and make "calling" sounds to let people know they would like some fish.*

Strandings

Although it is normal for the bodies of dead animals to be washed ashore, the sight of dead whales or dolphins lying on our beaches usually worries us. We are even more concerned when we are told that many of the animals seem to deliberately strand themselves and often resist our efforts to save them.

Death in the ocean

Just like land animals, animals living in the sea die of old age, disease, or other natural causes. Some of the bodies will be washed ashore with the tide, while most will decay in the sea. This is normal in nature.

However, sometimes you will read or hear about dolphins or porpoises swimming to shore and stranding themselves, and eventually dying of heat and stress.

These mysterious strandings also happened in ancient times, when records show that dolphins and porpoises stranded themselves onshore. Like today, they sometimes died alone, with another dolphin, or in a large group of between 20 and 30 dolphins. It is only in recent years that scientists have been able to find out some of the reasons for this behavior.

Scientific explanations

Many theories have been suggested as to why dolphins and porpoises strand themselves. Some say their sonar system gets confused, or that parasites enter their ears and upset their sonar echoes. Others suggest that noise from ships, water pollution, radar, television, radio transmissions, earthquakes, storms, or even phases of the moon upset them. But after studying these theories scientists have rejected all of them.

◀ *Dolphins or porpoises may be confused when they are gently lifted back into the water. Helpers can support them until they are able to swim freely by themselves.*

▼ *A helicopter is used to help rescuers herd dolphins back to the open ocean.*

Steve Dawson/Hedgehog House, New Zealand

The West Australian

Road accidents in the ocean

Scientists now believe that live strandings are similar to having a road accident, but at sea.

The earth has a magnetic field. It is determined by the magnetic features of the soil and rocks beneath the land surface or the ocean floor. Scientists think that dolphins and porpoises use their magnetic sense to "read" (like reading a map) these features as though they were "hills" (higher magnetic fields) and "valleys" (lower magnetic fields).

Q. Which types of dolphin and porpoise strand?

A. All species (except some river dolphins) have at some time been found stranded. Toothed whales from the open ocean strand together in large numbers more often than inshore species. This is because "offshore types" are very sociable animals that live in large groups. When any member of a herd becomes stranded, the others will follow it. As a result, many end up on the shore. False killer whales and the large dolphins (short-finned and long-finned pilot whales) are notorious for mass strandings.

These magnetic hills and valleys have been produced by the movements of the continents over millions of years. They form "paths" in the ocean like giant "freeways." When dolphins and porpoises travel on these freeways they know in which direction they are going because there is always a hill on one side and a valley on the other.

In some places, the hills and valleys are perpendicular (at right angles) to the coast. If dolphins and porpoises make a map-reading mistake, they may follow the freeways onto the coast and strand.

Do they try to get back on the freeway? Perhaps many of them do. The problem is we do not know exactly how often they get lost. Those we hear about are the ones that do not get back on the freeway. Possibly they are so shocked and exhausted by their mistake that they give up and do not even want humans to save them. Strandings remain a problem we still have to solve.

▼ *As their skin is very delicate, dolphins and porpoises should always be lifted in a sling or a stretcher, not pulled or pushed over the sand.*

Steven French

How to help a stranded dolphin or porpoise

If you find a stranded dolphin or porpoise, there are two things you can do:

1. Get help quickly by reporting the stranding to a police officer, the Coast Guard, life-guard, teacher, or the local tourist office.
2. Try to find out whether the animal is alive or dead. See if the eyes are open. If you are still not sure, stand well in front of it and listen for breathing. If it is alive, do not get too close as it may hit you with its tail.

When helpers arrive, they can assist the dolphin or porpoise by:

1. Keeping it cool, calm, and comfortable. The animal's skin is very delicate and must not dry out, so keeping it damp with a wet towel or some seaweed is a good idea. The animal's blowhole or eyes must never be covered.
2. Recording accurate details and measurements of the animal, such as its size, shape, color, and where it was found — even if the animal is dead.
3. Setting up a team system so that one team can fetch water, one team can keep people away and try to keep the animal calm, and one team can organize food for the helpers who will be cold, tired, and hungry.

Only an expert can decide how or if a dolphin or porpoise can be returned to the water, or whether the animal is in pain and must be destroyed. If he or she decides to return the animal to the water, the helpers must take care not to pull its flippers. Always push the animal on its side or at the bottom of the dorsal fin. Better still, lift the animal in something like a big sling or stretcher. *Never* tow an animal behind a boat by the tail — it will drown!

If there are other dolphins and porpoises in the sea nearby, the helpers should try to stop them "following" the stranded animal by swimming ashore. They can do this by getting a group of people to stand close together in the shallow waters. They should also take a count of how many dolphins and porpoises are in the water, and record their size and color.

► *Pilot whales are well known for their mass strandings.*

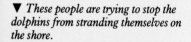
◄ *To save as many stranded animals as possible by returning them to the water quickly, a farm tractor or front-end loader can be used to carry them back into the ocean.*

▼ *These people are trying to stop the dolphins from stranding themselves on the shore.*

The West Australian

Simon Cowling / Horizon

▲ *Strandings have always interested people. This stranding took place in Cornwall, England.*

Dolphins and porpoises in captivity

It is wonderful to watch an animal in its natural environment. However, since early this century when scientists first saw how dolphins and porpoises were being killed for food and sport, efforts have been made to study and keep them in captivity for future generations.

The first dolphins to be put on public display were five belukhas that were shipped to England in 1870. In 1913 at the Battery Aquarium in New York, bottlenose dolphins and harbor porpoises were exhibited for the first time. Animals rescued from live strandings were occasionally displayed in the 1930s in Plymouth, England, but it was not until 1962

Marineland of Florida

◄ *Adolph Frohn was the world's first dolphin trainer. Here he is working with a dolphin called Flippy at Marine Studios, Florida, in 1942.*

▼ *Today, many dolphins and porpoises, such as these bottlenose dolphins, are kept in large salt-water pools or enclosed parts of the sea, called oceanariums.*

Did you know?

The water in which captive dolphins and porpoises live must be checked constantly. It must be very clean, and the salt level has to be maintained at a certain level. The skin of dolphins and porpoises is very sensitive. It will form ulcers if water conditions are not just right.

when two female bottlenose dolphins were obtained that the animals became permanent exhibits.

The dolphins that really excited human interest were those photographed at Marine Studios in St Augustine, Florida, in 1938. They became such a popular attraction that the studio began training them, and for the first time dolphin behavior was studied.

From 1939 to 1963, 27 dolphins were born in captivity at Marine Studios. The first orcas were captured and kept in captivity at Seattle Aquarium, Washington, in 1964.

According to current records, at least 2,700 bottlenose dolphins have been taken into captivity worldwide. Also being held in captivity are about 150 spotted dolphins, 120 orcas, 100 belukhas, more than 80 harbor porpoises, numerous common dolphins, Amazon River dolphins, finless porpoises, and a few Chinese river dolphins.

▶ *An orca in captivity shows the crowd how high it can leap.*

▼ *Bottlenose dolphins at Marine World, Florida.*

What we learn

By observing dolphins and porpoises in captivity, scientists have learned how they breed, how their senses work, how they echolocate, how they dive, and how they interact with one another.

Recent studies carried out at the Seven Seas Panorama of Brookfield, Chicago, have enabled scientists to work out how dolphins listen to ultrasonic pulses for echolocation. They found that the lower jaw is very important in this behavior.

The bottlenose dolphin was one of the first to be held in captivity and it adapted to captive conditions very quickly. This means scientists know a lot about its social interactions. Dolphins seem to rank themselves by size and sex, with the large males leading the group. They also pair off, but it is the mother and child that swim together, not the mother and father.

Did you know?

Dolphins are very good at imitating behavior. One female bottlenose, in the Port Elizabeth Oceanarium in South Africa, imitated the behavior of a young male fur seal that was in the same tank. The bottlenose began to swim like a seal, lying on her side with one flipper out of the water. She also began to scratch herself with her flippers in the same way the seal groomed himself. She mimicked the seal asleep, by swimming on her back, flippers pressed flat against her belly.

▼ *Bottlenose dolphins are playful and friendly and love being fed fresh fish.*

Ben Cropp

► *Some people believe that dolphins should not be taught to perform acts for audiences. But most "acts" are natural behaviors. Training an animal only means it will then perform these acts on command.*

Over the years much has been learned about the best way to house and feed dolphins and porpoises. Because they spend all their time in water, it must be constantly cleaned and kept at the right salt level.

Although some scientists argue that an animal studied in captivity does not give an accurate picture of how the same animal would behave in its natural world, captivity has helped broaden our understanding of these animals. Hopefully this awareness will help the survival of dolphins and porpoises in the wild.

Did you know?

Captivity makes strange companions! This orca and Pacific white-sided dolphin would be enemies in the wild. The orca would prey on and attack the dolphin for food. But, in captivity, they have become best friends.

Glossary

BAIJI — Means "white dolphin" in Chinese and is the name given to the Chinese river dolphin. It is one of the twelve most endangered species in the world.

BLOWHOLE — The single opening on the top of dolphins' and porpoises' heads. They breathe in and out through it when they surface.

DORSAL FIN — The back fin used for steering. It has tough fibers inside it to hold it erect. Dorsal fins come in a variety of shapes and sizes. They can be sickle-shaped, triangular, or bluntly rounded. In some species, for example the finless porpoise, they are missing altogether.

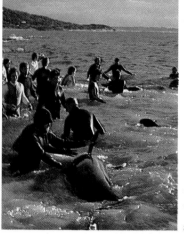

ECHOLOCATION — A special sense that allows dolphins and porpoises to "see" with sound. They use it to navigate and get information about their surroundings.

EVOLUTION — The slow changes that have occurred in living things since life began on earth.

FAMILY — A scientific grouping. True dolphins belong to the family Delphinidae. Porpoises belong to the family Phocoenidae.

FLIPPERS — The two side fins. They are broad flat forelimbs that are used for steering and balance.

GENUS — A smaller scientific group than family or order. Animals belonging to the same genus have certain features in common.

INCIDENTAL KILLINGS — When deaths occur as the result of something else, for example, when dolphins get trapped in nets cast out to catch tuna. Many dolphins die this way.

MAMMAL — Refers to a large scientific group. It includes humans, dogs, whales, dolphins, and porpoises. All mammals are warm-blooded, breathe air, and feed their young on milk from mammary glands.

MELON — The large mound on the foreheads of dolphins and porpoises. It is an essential part of the echolocation system. The fat it contains responds to sound vibrations that are then interpreted by the brain.

ORDER — A large scientific group. Whales, dolphins, and porpoises belong to the order Cetacea.

PURSE-SEINES — The huge nets used to catch tuna.

SPECIES — A group of individuals that have features in common. They are able to breed together to produce live, fertile young.

SPY-HOPPING — When dolphins balance on their tails and raise themselves up out of the water to look around.

VORTEX — The whirlpool effect created by dolphins and porpoises when they move their tails up and down in the water.

List of scientific names

Dolphins and porpoises are usually referred to by their common names: for example, the bottlenose dolphin and the harbor porpoise. The scientific names for dolphins and porpoises are made up of two parts, like your first name and surname. The first part is the genus (or group) to which the animal belongs, for example, the white-beaked dolphin belongs to the genus *Lagenorhynchus*. The second part of the scientific name is the species name.

The scientific names listed below are for all the dolphins and porpoises mentioned in this book.

Common name	Scientific name
Amazon River dolphin	*Inia geoffrensis*
Baird's beaked whale	*Berardius bairdii*
belukha	*Delphinapterus leucas*
bottlenose dolphin	*Tursiops truncatus*
Burmeister's porpoise	*Phocoena spinipinnis*
Chinese river dolphin (baiji)	*Lipotes vexillifer*
Commerson's dolphin	*Cephalorhynchus commersonii*
common dolphin	*Delphinus delphis*
Dall's porpoise	*Phocoenoides dalli*
dusky dolphin	*Lagenorhynchus obscurus*
false killer whale	*Pseudorca crassidens*
finless porpoise	*Neophocaena phocaenoides*
franciscana	*Pontoporia blainvillei*
Ganges River dolphin	*Platanista gangetica*
giant bottlenose whale	*Berardius bairdii*
gray grampus	*Grampus griseus*
harbor porpoise	*Phocoena phocoena*
hourglass dolphin	*Lagenorhynchus cruciger*
Indo-Pacific humpback dolphin	*Sousa chinensis*
Irrawaddy dolphin	*Orcaella brevirostris*
narwhal	*Monodon monoceros*
orca	*Orcinus orca*
Pacific white-sided dolphin	*Lagenorhynchus obliquidens*
pantropical spotted dolphin	*Stenella attenuata*
Risso's dolphin	*Grampus griseus*
rough-toothed dolphin	*Steno bredanensis*
spectacled porpoise	*Australophocoena dioptrica*
strap-toothed whale	*Mesoplodon layardii*
striped dolphin	*Stenella coeruleoalba*
vaquita	*Phocoena sinus*
white-beaked dolphin	*Lagenorhynchus albirostris*

Peter Corkeron

Hugh Edwards

Paul Ensor

Frans Lanting/Bruce Coleman Ltd

Index